God created grief as a way for us to value life, value each other, and process the pain of losing someone valuable in our lives. Without grief, we would not appreciate life. It is a painful, gut-wrenching, and often ugly process, but it is necessary, to heal and to fully appreciate God's creation and His many blessings for us. "Forever Changed" demonstrates the grief process in a respectful and direct way that people who are grieving and those supporting them can appreciate. It was an honor to read it, and I know God will use it to bring healing to many, many people.

Melissa Finger,
Master of Science in Marriage and Family Therapy,
National Certified Counselor, Biblical Counselor

FOREVER CHANGED
My Journey from Grief to Joy

Debbie McClure

Foreword *by Dirk McClure*

Copyright © 2012 by Debbie McClure

Forever Changed: My Journey from Grief to Joy

by Debbie McClure

Printed in the United States of America

ISBN 978-1-470106-72-0

All rights reserved solely by the author. The author guarantees all contents are original and do not infringe upon the legal rights of any other person or work, and that this book is not libelous, plagiarized, or in any other way illegal. If any portion of this book is fictitious, the author guarantees it does not represent any real event or person in a way that could be deemed libelous. No part of this book may be reproduced in any form without the permission of the author.

The Scripture versions cited in this book are identified in Appendix 1, which hereby becomes a part of this copyright page.

https://www.facebook.com/foreverchangedbook

foreverchangedbook@gmail.com

TABLE OF CONTENTS

	Foreword *by Dirk McClure*	vii
	Introduction	xi
	Acknowledgements	xvii
1:	**We'll Never Pass This Way Again**	1
2:	**Final Months, Days, Moments**	5
3:	**Asleep, Awake**	19
4:	**Remembering Mama**	23
5:	**Surviving the Firsts**	43
6:	**Lynnaya**	61
7:	**Always in My Thoughts**	67
8:	**Moving Forward**	75
9:	**Spiritual Growth**	83
10:	**Receiving Help *from* Others**	91
11:	**Being There *for* Others**	101
12:	**Searching …**	107
13:	**Healing …**	111
14:	**And Still Learning**	119
15:	**The Question of Heaven**	123
	The Bible on Heaven	131
16:	**Relationship with Jesus**	137
	The Bible on Death and Resurrection	151
	Comfort from Scripture	155

Appendix 1: *Scripture Version Copyrights*
Appendix 2: *Index of Debbie's Poems*

Foreword
by Dirk McClure

"I never thought I could hurt this much." That's what my wife, Debbie, told me the day her mother died. She held me tightly and cried throughout the night. I had never witnessed her sobbing quite that intensely. I had never seen her quite that broken. And I had never felt quite so useless.

By nature, I'm a problem solver. Who doesn't love to see something fixed? As Debbie grieved the loss of her mother, I actually struggled with some feelings of my own. I felt that I wasn't doing enough for her. I wanted to help her feel better. I wanted to make the hurting stop. Unfortunately, her pain was something that I couldn't take away. This was something I couldn't fix.

As supporters, we genuinely desire to comfort close friends or family members who have experienced loss. However, in our rush to convey the perfect little phrase or the wisest spiritual insight, our words can often ring hollow while the encounter turns awkward. Despite our best intentions to help, when it comes to what we say, sometimes less is more. A simple hug and a sincere "I'm sorry" are better than overdoing it.

I've found that one of the best things we can do for someone experiencing a painful loss is to simply *be there* for them, to be available. It's also incredibly important to keep the lines of communication open. Then, at the appropriate time, we can offer our support in ways that are truly needed and can be received. Sometimes, the best way to help is by meeting a practical need, like providing a meal.

With Debbie, there was a tricky balance between staying close and being available, while also giving her the space she needed to process things on her own. Even though I felt that I wasn't helping much at the time, she later told me how much she appreciated, not only my availability, but the fact that I didn't try to give pat answers or go for the quick fix.

One thing I did was to let Debbie know that we were in this together. I shared my appreciation of her mother through meaningful memories. It comforted her to know that we were both sharing the loss. It also became a surprisingly healthy outlet for us to recall humorous stories together. There are times when it's okay to laugh through the tears.

I watched my wife gain ground steadily, but there were moments, even years after her mother died, when the pain became intense again. It's important for supporters to be available for the long haul. When someone loses a person who was an integral part of his or her life, the pain can show up in a variety of forms and linger for many years.

The book you hold in your hands documents my wife's journey through the grief of losing her mom. A large portion of this book is made up of the deeply personal writings Debbie penned during her season of grief. In remarkably candid and transparent fashion, she shares her lowest lows, raw feelings, key breakthroughs, and her eventual restoration to God's fullness of joy.

Everyone's journey is different. This book is certainly not an instruction manual on the right way to get through the grieving process. While there are some unhealthy expressions of grief, there is no singular right way to grieve. Debbie's desire in publishing her story is that it will be a source of hope for others experiencing the loss of a loved one. We also think it can be an insightful resource for those who want to be better equipped to comfort others experiencing a difficult loss.

Introduction

I have always been an inquisitive person. I was the child who pelted her parents with "why questions" *all the time.*

I am a very detail-oriented person. I don't like surprises. I like to be aware of what's going on with me internally, as well as what's happening around me. I'm just naturally curious.

I think it's in my DNA to know all I possibly can about topics that interest me. I spent two years planning my wedding, researching every detail. In my spare time, I spend hours doing research into my family history for fun. I read several books every month; there are always stacks of them on my night stand. I am, admittedly, an information geek.

When my mother died, I treated her death much like I treated other events in my life. I tried to obtain as much information as possible to ascertain and process what I was going through internally. I also did a great deal of research about heaven, Mom's final destination.

I woke up one morning, about three and a half years after Mom's death, with a Scripture song in my head—Robert Manzano's "Beauty for Ashes." The lyrics are from the book of Isaiah.

> To appoint unto them that mourn in Zion, to give unto them beauty for ashes, the oil of joy for mourning, the garment of praise for the spirit of heaviness; that they might be called trees of righteousness, the planting of the LORD, that He might be glorified. *Isaiah 61:3 (KJV)*

I decided to do a little research *(naturally)* about what each of the phrases in this verse means. What I found fascinated me. I found two of the phrases most interesting; "the oil of joy for mourning" and "the garment of praise for the spirit of heaviness."

When I looked up the first phrase, I found an encouraging explanation from C. H. Spurgeon, a preacher and author who lived in the 1800's. In one of his sermons—"No. 1016, delivered at Metropolitan Tabernacle, Newington"—he explained that, in the Oriental culture, during times of great joy, perfumed oils were lavishly poured on people to honor and esteem them. He related that "the Holy Spirit comes upon those who believe in Jesus, and gives them an anointing of perfume, most precious, more sweet and costly than the herd of Arab."

So, instead of mourning, Christians receive the Holy Spirit's anointing. The Holy Spirit, the Comforter, then reveals the things of Christ and makes us "not merely glad, but honored and esteemed."

I continued my research, looking into the phrase "the garment of praise for the spirit of heaviness." Spurgeon's sermon yielded even more encouragement for me. "Jesus Christ will cover you, and the sordid garments of your woe shall be put aside for the brilliant array of delight." He explained that it would be a fair trade to exchange the spirit of heaviness for the spirit of praise, but, "as your heaviness you tried to keep to yourself, so your praise you shall not keep to yourself. It shall be a garment to you, external and visible, as well as inward and profound." His interpretation was that people will see that God has done great things for you, as if they were on display.

It was after reading about the comfort of God's Spirit, which I had experienced first-hand, and reading how the garment of praise is not meant to be kept to ourselves but displayed to others, that I sensed God nudging me to write this book. I felt totally inadequate, but decided to take the steps of putting together my thoughts, feelings, and emotions and see what God would do through them. I began by combining the research I had done with very personal poems I had written since Mom's death. My goal was to share my journey through the depths of mourning to the joy that exists on the other side.

At first, my intention was only to share my *story in book form* with family members and close friends. However, the more I thought and prayed about it, the more I felt God calling me to share my journey with a much wider audience: anyone needing encouragement over a loss, and the people who love them and want to comfort them in their grief. My heart aches when I hear that someone has lost a person they love, especially a parent, spouse, or child.

As I continued to organize my poems, stories, and recollections, I thought about how one day my own daughters will have to deal with their mother's death. I desperately wanted to share my heart in a way that could make their individual journeys a little bit easier. I hope I can give them the assurance that they will never be alone.

As I wrote, there were times that the sorrow would come back so strongly that I couldn't write any more. I would cry out to God, "This hurts too much." Yet, in a still, quiet way, I always sensed God's gentle direction to keep writing.

Some of the writing was done when raw emotion was the only outlet for my grief. It's tempting to not be transparent, but it's important to show those strong feelings. People need to know it's normal to feel that way from time to time.

The process of writing has brought me tears and healing, confusion and clarity, and comforting therapy.

For me, the grief and healing processes took place in a cyclical manner. As you read my story, you'll more-than-likely pick up on this. Time frames will feel scattered; thoughts will seem to jump back and forth. Everyone would love to follow a simple, straight-forward path in their journey through grief, but that's not the way it happens. It's more like an unnerving swirl of emotions, crazy turns, and curves.

I've learned that everyone grieves differently. In this book, I'm definitely not suggesting to anyone how they should get through it. There really is no one right way to grieve. I'm simply sharing *my journey* through it. As you walk with me through my story, I hope you, too, will come to know that you are not alone.

Finally, I say this to those of you who may be grieving right now, as you begin to read this book.

I have a word of caution for you. "Forever Changed" may trigger feelings in a deeper way than you might expect. It's okay if that happens. If you are triggered, in any way, by reading this book, please be careful to move forward at a more comfortable pace. Maybe you can allow the book to help you process your pain. You might need to take a break from it instead, and come back when your grief has been processed a little more.

I've been where you find yourself now. My heart breaks over the fact that you have to travel this road. Let me share with you my journey, and the words of hope that I received along the way. They might very well bring you comfort, along with a new sense that God can lead you through the grieving process and fill your life with joy. This is my heart-felt prayer for you.

Acknowledgements

Many family members and friends have encouraged me throughout the process of writing "Forever Changed." Several were directly involved in making it a reality.

My brother, Donnie Wells, walked this journey with me on so many levels; from sharing in my grief like no one else possibly could, to tirelessly reading every word I wrote. I knew I always had his full support. My heartfelt thanks to him. No one could ask for a better cheerleader.

Marina McClure, my sister-in-law, and Diane McClure, my mother-in-law, spent hours editing rough drafts. Their encouragement, candid advice, and listening ears helped give me the drive I needed to transfer my ideas from my heart to the printed page.

Our friend Eric Holmes provided the comprehensive and final edits of this project. He worked, with meticulous detail, to take my raw narrative and turn it into the book that it has become. His insights, perspective, and creative suggestions were invaluable.

My thanks to everyone who read draft copies of the book, offering insight and final suggestions. This book was made better because of them.

Dirk, my wonderful husband, has been there with me throughout the entire process. What started as a personal journal would never have made it to book form without his vision, encouragement, persistence, and overall support. I feel so blessed that God gave him to me. God's design for our lives together makes me forever grateful.

Most of all, I am thankful to God for taking me on the life-changing, healing journey of putting my thoughts and feelings into words that can help others. Father God, You are my comfort, my strength, my joy, and the lifter of my head.

Debbie McClure, April 2012

FOREVER CHANGED

Chapter 1
We'll Never Pass This Way Again

> *"I expect to pass through this world but once.*
> *Any good, therefore, that I can do*
> *or any kindness I can show to any fellow creature,*
> *let me do it now.*
> *Let me not defer or neglect it*
> *for I shall not pass this way again."*
> *– generally credited to Stephen Grellet,*
> *but without proven attribution*

She was usually referring to a family vacation or a fun event. I can still hear my mother's voice, calling me by her pet name for me. "Sis, we'll never pass this way again."

There was a sense about Mom that she appreciated all of life's moments, the big ones and the small ones alike, savoring them like the last few bites of dessert. When I was in college I thought that philosophy was old-fashioned. While Mom was all about "enjoying the journey," I was more goal-oriented. I guess I wasn't as interested in stopping and smelling the roses because I was too concerned about getting to the other side of the garden.

Mom's zest for living life to its fullest probably came from lessons she learned through losses she experienced in her early adult life. She lost so many loved ones in such a short period of time.

She lost her mother to lymphoma in 1965. My grandmother was only 41 years old; my mom was 22 then. Mom was the oldest of seven children, five of whom were still living at home at the time.

In 1967, two of her brothers were killed in a car accident. They were only 18 and 21.

Then, the most painful loss, the most life-changing loss came in December 1968. My young mother and father lost their darling Diana Elaine, who was just two months old. Mom always referred to losing their baby girl as the turning point in their lives. It was in those trying times that she committed her life to Jesus Christ, and never turned back.

Her journey through grief was not an easy one. Mom used to tell me that she really couldn't remember how she made it through those first few months. Caring for David, her only child at that time, was her main motivation during that time. Even though she was always a good mama, I just can't imagine dealing with the losses that she walked through during those dark years.

The doctor told my parents they might not be able to have any more children, but God blessed them with three more: Danny, Donnie, and me. Her testimony was that "God always blesses us beyond our own understanding."

She found Jesus when she was at her lowest, and emerged a joyful person who was full of fun and life. That's the mark of a life touched by the comfort of God.

* * * * * * *

It's said that "into each life some rain must fall." My downpour took place on December 1st, 2004, when my second pregnancy ended in a miscarriage.

I wished for you,
But you never came—
A gift from heaven … postponed.

I've cried my tears.
I've felt my pain.
But in my heart I know
You're heaven's gain.

The years will fly.
We'll try again.
Even with new joys
Your memory will stand.

Life goes on;
Sad but true.
God gives us strength
To get us through.

I want to hold you.
That can't happen now.
It's hard to wait,
Knowing that someday
I'll finally get to see your face.

Love, Mama

When I called with the sad news, Mom offered to drive the 250 miles between us to comfort me. I insisted that she didn't need to do that. Two weeks later, Mom went in for emergency intestinal surgery, and it was my turn to wish away the distance between us.

Christmas was very different that year. I remember the feeling of *finally* getting to my parents' house. Mom held me and we cried together. Although we talked on the phone nearly every day, it was the first time I had seen her since the two events had happened.

Because of Mom's recovery from the surgery, she couldn't do much in regard to her normal Christmas preparations. My sisters-in-law and I prepared the meal for everyone while Mom slept.

She slept a lot during that visit.

Chapter 2
Final Months, Days, Moments

Mom paid my family and me an extended visit the following April. She had gained 50 pounds since Christmas, and wasn't feeling well the entire time she was with us. She was in so much pain that my husband Dirk and I kept pleading with her to go to the doctor. But she kept telling us that it was just minor digestive issues from her intestinal surgery. As we tried to convince her that something might be wrong, she tried to convince us that everything was okay. She mentioned something about abnormal test results and ER doctors recommending a specialist, but she was sure they were wrong. She was so convincing that I dismissed it. However, what Mom didn't tell us was that blood tests revealed elevated levels of CA125 protein. High concentrations of this protein indicate the presence of tumor cells.

Mom had an incredibly high tolerance for pain, but the weekend after her visit with us, she finally let Dad take her to the hospital. Immediately, they began her first round of chemotherapy. Malignant, water-producing tumors had invaded her lung and stomach areas in clusters.

* * * * * * *

Mom's family reunion was held in June each year. She and I attended many of them together, missing only a few. Mom was weak, but she wanted to go to this reunion very much. She asked me to take her. In years past, Mom would drive four and a half hours from her home in south central Missouri to Kansas City, where I lived. Then, we would split up the rest of the eight-hour drive to her hometown, near Mitchell, South Dakota. This time, Dad drove her to my house and I drove the rest of the way. I didn't realize at the time how thankful I would be for that trip.

Our Last Ride

I didn't know it then—
That it would be our last ride
Across the prairie you love;
Seeing sights that made up
Part of your history.

We rode past the old home place.
We had gone there many times before,
But it seemed different that visit,
Like you were saying goodbye.

We rode past your old one-room school house.
You took pride in telling stories,
Uniquely yours,
Of a time that has passed.

We drove by the town
That was your Saturday night place—
A town that time has forgotten.
But you never did.

We made visits to those whom you love;
You touched so many in your lifetime.
Your energy was low,
But love was fueling you.

Many times before
I had heard the tales,
But I didn't stop you.
I liked hearing them again and again.
It gave insight as to the person you were.

You were taken from this prairie land,
Not by choice, but by a parental drawing;
Much like the way
You were taken from this earth.

You always had two worlds
Pulling you for different reasons.
You lived in one
And could always visit the other.

I didn't know it then—
That it would be our last ride.

Those are sweet memories for me.

* * * * * * *

That summer was a very busy time for us. We put our starter home up for sale and were doing a lot of showings. We were also looking for a larger home for our family. I was pregnant again, but having a rough time physically. I didn't travel much during those months.

Meanwhile, Mom's doctors were trying several types of chemotherapy with her—first IVs, then pills. The treatments seemed to be working at first and the CA125 numbers were going down. All the while, Mom's faith in God remained very strong, even when it began to look like the cancer treatments were no longer working and her health began to decline.

When we visited her over the Labor Day weekend, I was shocked at how physically different she looked. For the first time, she looked old to me. Her hair was thin and gray, and she looked frail, although her spunky spirit and attitude were still intact.

Mom may have been trying to prepare me for the worst that weekend. She showed me all of her bank account information. Because she was a real estate agent and owned rental property, she walked me through her files and showed me how she did her bookkeeping. I didn't think of it as *Mom getting things in order*; just that I was helping her out until she regained her strength.

A few weeks later, right after her 63rd birthday, Mom came to see us in our new house. Because she wanted to see the new place so badly, she talked Dad into making the trip, even though she should have stayed at home to rest.

Again, I was taken aback by how difficult simple activities had become for her. There were two steps that led into the house from the garage, and it took Mom more than a few minutes to painfully navigate each one. She couldn't walk up the stairs to see our bedrooms, so she sat on a chair at the base of the stairway and asked questions about the layout and details of the rooms. She said she wanted to *see* the house so she could picture me in it when we were talking on the phone.

After that visit, it seemed that Mom was getting weaker. In October, I decided that my 2½-year-old daughter, Lynnaya, and I would spend some time helping Mom out around the house. It was hard for her to keep up with her rental management duties, so I worked on that for her as well. It seemed to lift her spirits to have us there.

My brother Donnie drove from Florida to see her in mid-October. He, too, saw that Mom was losing strength.

At the end of October, Mom called each one of her children and leveled with us.

"Sis, the doctors have tried everything they can to save my life. And even though there are some old chemotherapy drugs they can try, they've pretty much said that there's not much hope."

How in the world is a daughter supposed to process words like those from her mother? My heart sank, and I felt like a deflated balloon. We cried together over the phone.

For the first time, all of those little doubts I had been able to keep on the outer edges of my mind came crashing into one big fear that Mom could actually die. And there it was, after all this time — the word *die*.

Mom told me that she didn't want her life to be over. She wanted to meet the new baby. We cried for a long time together. There were words at the end of the conversation about "faith that God could give us a miracle" and "what a wonderful testimony this could be," but the shock and the pain were fresh. I cried so much that night that my eyes and my throat hurt.

I brought Lynnaya with me again when I returned to Mom's at the beginning of November. At that point, she needed a lot of assistance and it was taxing my dad, being her primary caregiver, to do everything she needed to have done.

Mom had a dream during this time that prompted a new kind of preparation. She dreamed that my brother, Danny, and his wife, Amy, were with her as she was dying. (At that time, they were serving as missionaries in Africa.)

When she woke up, she called my cousin Bryan, a funeral director, to get those plans together.

She also sat me and my sister-in-law Anita down and told us how she wanted some of her possessions to be distributed among the family members after she was gone. We labeled the items accordingly.

At one point, when she was choosing songs to be played at her funeral, I started crying. The moment was just too overwhelming.

"Why are you crying?" she asked.

"This is all just too hard to think about."

As funeral plans continued to be made, I began to be irritated by the fact that everyone thought we needed to do this now. *Denial* was starting to manifest.

Mom got firm, and said, "Listen to me, Sis. I know this is hard. But when I'm gone, you'll appreciate knowing that you did things exactly like I wanted."

I stayed at Mom's for a little more than a week. During that time, a home medical supply company had come and set up oxygen, to help ease her breathing.

By November 12th, Mom's breathing was growing more and more difficult, and the pain from the tumors in her stomach had become unbearable.

We had learned that the hospital there in her small town wasn't equipped to handle the care Mom needed, so we called an ambulance service from a nearby town to take Mom to the hospital in Columbia, Missouri, about two hours away.

While we waited, my brother called some of his friends at the fire department to help carry Mom to the ambulance, due to her body size and the fact that she was now unable to walk on her own. We moved furniture to clear a path for the stretcher between the front door and her bedroom. For 45 minutes to an hour, everything seemed to play out like a movie in slow motion. The whole scene was completely overwhelming.

The ambulance arrived, and they started moving Mom out of the house. That's when I lost it. I could no longer control my emotions. It was another of those few times in the process when I had to face the fact that she might not make it. My mind was swirling.

"Who is Debbie?" an EMT called out. "She wants to talk to Debbie."

Despite the pain that she was in, and the commotion of getting her into the ambulance, Mom would not let the vehicle pull away without talking to me first. I appeared at the door with tears streaming down my cheeks and a big lump in my throat.

"It'll be okay, whichever way it goes," she said. "You'll know where I'll be. I know where I'm going, and I'm not afraid."

I cried harder. She told me to wipe my tears and be strong.

"Okay, Mama. I love you."

Then, in her firm, motherly tone, she said, "Stop crying."

The ambulance pulled away and we all followed behind it. I guess I thought that every ambulance ride was a dramatic race to the hospital, with sirens and lights and the whole bit. But we drove the speed limit the whole two hours to Columbia. No lights, no police escort, nothing like that. As a matter of fact, it seemed more like a funeral procession as our three-car convoy followed the ambulance.

We later learned that one of the EMTs in the ambulance was a Spirit-filled Christian man. He prayed with Mom, and put her at ease during the trip. I am always so grateful when God places just the right people in our path at just the right time.

We spent some time with Mom in her room that night. My dad was there, along with my oldest brother, David, and his daughter, Kaytlyn, as well as Dirk, Lynnaya and me. There was a point in the evening when Mom called everyone to her bedside because she had some things she wanted to discuss with us.

She spoke to Dad first.

"If I don't get my miracle, I want you to go on with your life, and find someone else to share it with. Only ... choose someone who will be good to the children and grandchildren."

Then, a smile softly appeared.

"Because if the roles were reversed, I would definitely get myself a boyfriend."

It was nice to see a reminder of her sense of humor.

She asked us all if we had released her, or if we were still holding on to her, "because," she said, "I wake up each morning surprised that I'm still alive."

Each of us assured her that we were still praying for a miracle, but had released her if it was God's will to take her home. I wondered if, on the inside, she was holding on to see Danny and Amy once more. They were facing a lot of obstacles in getting permission to leave Africa for a return trip to the United States.

I stayed with Mom for awhile at the hospital, until she sent me home to "take a break" for a few days. My brother David also spent time with her at the hospital during her stay. When it was determined that Mom should return home, she asked her good friend, Martha, to come and stay with her at the house.

TO: Close friends
FROM: Debbie
DATE: 11/17/05

[On Sunday, I] returned from spending 10 days with my mom. Things aren't looking good for her. The doctors have tried four different kinds of chemo with no success to dry up her tumors, and they have no other alternatives to try. Mom has stood firm, believing for a miracle since she was diagnosed with ovarian cancer. She realizes that God's ways are not always our ways, and He may choose to take her home for the *ultimate healing* instead of an earthly one. She is completely bedridden at this point. Please keep her, and our entire family, in your prayers.

Danny and Amy are desperately trying to come home from Africa, but have run into problems with permits and visas to return, so it is still pending the decisions of officials. Hopefully, they'll be home by the weekend.

Our hearts are heavy, but we know it's in God's hands now. We'd love a healing miracle, but are prepared for that to not be the way God chooses to answer us.

Thanks for your love, friendship, and prayers.
Debbie

Martha took good care of Mom's physical needs at home. She read the Bible to her, prayed with her, and just let Mom be herself. (For that, we will forever be thankful.)

I stayed connected to Mom via telephone, calling her several times during that week at home. There were times when it was difficult for her to speak, so she would begin the conversation by saying, "You talk."

Sometimes it was just small talk, or I would catch her up on stories about her granddaughter. But there were also times when words just wouldn't come, and we would spend time just being quiet together. I told her I loved her often. I didn't know how much time she might have left, but I felt blessed to be able to tell her how much she meant to me. I can't imagine how extremely hard it must be when a loved one is taken suddenly, and there are no carefully-chosen last words or goodbyes.

At the end of the week, we learned that Danny and Amy would be able to come home from Africa after all, and that they would get in late Friday night. I told Mom that I would let them enjoy her company alone over the weekend, and that I would come and see her on Monday. She wouldn't have it. My brother Donnie was driving in from Florida, and she wanted all of her children to be together with her. So I decided to drive to Salem on Friday, November 18th.

Packing for that trip was very difficult. Although I was still praying for a miracle, I packed funeral clothes for my daughter and myself.

Mom could barely speak by the time I arrived. Asking for her granddaughter, she whispered, "Where's my baby girl?"

Lynnaya sat on the bed for a few minutes, but began to look a little frightened. Mom motioned for me to move her away, to protect her from sad memories I'm sure.

As we settled in for the evening, I volunteered for the 4 AM to 8 AM shift at Mom's bedside—a time to hold her hand, kiss her cheek, and whisper words of peace and comfort, a time to shed quiet tears and pray silent prayers.

I was pretty sleepy when Dad came in at eight to sit with Mom. Sometimes, I wish I would have stayed in the room. Forty-five minutes later, my mother slipped into the arms of her Lord and Savior.

Where's my baby girl? They were the last words I heard from Mom's lips. How fitting. She was crazy about her grandchildren.

I was prepared but in the *Denial* stage, so her death was still a shock. My family and I believed that Mom would be healed, but we didn't get the miracle we had been praying for. I hated to see her go, but was glad she wasn't suffering anymore. There were a lot of mixed emotions, but one thing I knew for sure: Mom stood firm in her faith to the end.

> I have fought the good fight, I have finished the race, I have kept the faith. *2 Timothy 4:7 (NIV)*

> Blessed is the one who perseveres under trial because, having stood the test, that person will

> receive the crown of life that the Lord has promised to those who love Him. *James 1:12 (NIV)*

I called my husband Dirk, who was back home in Kansas City. I could barely get the words out. He rushed to Salem to be with us.

Dirk held me in his arms through the entire night, and I cried through most of it. The sting of death was almost more than I could bear. I remember telling him that I didn't think it was going to be *this* hard.

With Lynnaya camped out on the floor beside us, I managed to get a little bit of sleep ... *finally*.

Chapter 3
Asleep, Awake

I woke up from a nap one day, when I was very young, and searched the entire house, calling out for my mom. She didn't answer. As I was getting more and more concerned — scared is more like it — I walked out the back door and saw that she was hanging clothes on the clothesline to dry.

I ran right into her arms, crying, "Oh, Mama! I thought you *leaveded* me."

As she held me, tears came to her eyes. "When the leaving is done, baby, you'll be the one doing it."

The Girl in My Life
(by Patty Larson Wells — "Mama")

Tonight, my child, you would not sleep. So I decided to be the self-indulgent mother, and I brought you to my bed.

You immediately discovered my book hidden under the pillow. Being a wiser, older mother than your brothers had, I can watch and enjoy you in a way I never could with them. So I let you play with one of my "beloved books."

As I watched, you struggled determinedly till you were the possessor of the book. I lay there thinking of your future, and wondered if you would work as hard at possessing life.

You beat aimlessly, as a little one will when things don't go their way. You rested your head, but soon began again. As life moves in the wrong direction, will you remember to rest and try again, or will you give up?

Then you bent a page, and I wondered, Will I stand by and watch you wrongfully bend your life, or will I try to intervene, as I did with my book?

God grant that I have the strength to let you bend and unbend your life after my years of instruction have passed. In so doing, you will learn.

You passed up page after page as you searched for one to chew on, while I knew full well the first one would be as good as the last. Will I be able to watch you pass up young men, afraid of who you will choose and what lifestyle will be yours?

You turned the book aside, flopping aimlessly on your tummy. Will life hold your interest, or will you glide aimlessly through it?

Finally, you chewed your selected page, leaving your prints and teeth marks in my book. What marks will you leave in life? How many times will I run interference? Will I stand by and let life teach you? And oh, how many times will I not be there to know?

If I could only keep you as close as you are tonight, my ten-month-old, and, yet, let you turn the pages of life alone – to live, to learn, to grow.

I pray to my Maker to help you and me in our lives together – apart. This is all I can do, my little one.

As I began to stir the morning after Mom died—for just a second or two—what had happened didn't register. But as I became more awake, I realized that my childhood worries were just as real for me at 33 as they were when I was a little girl.

I cooked the Thanksgiving meal.
I'm sure it didn't taste as good as yours.
At least the turkey wasn't dry.
You've taught me some needed skills.

I cried the night before
As I sat rocking my little one,
Because of the reality of what is,
And because of what's to come.

You should have been humming,
As you often did, in the kitchen.
The smell of baking pies was missing,
As if no one thought or cared.

I tried my best to remember
How you showed me to do things.
I even let my daughter help;
The traditions must go on.

FOREVER CHANGED

*I know you cannot hear me
Or see me cry my tears,
But if you could, you'd see
That I'm facing all those fears.*

*I'm moving on,
But that's so hard.
How did you do it
With the losses you had?*

*I'm finding I am stronger
Than I ever thought I could be,
And appreciating even more
Just how strong you must have been.*

*I love you, Mama.
I hope you are closer than I imagine,
But I want my girls to have their mom,
So, I have to stay here much longer.*

*You said when the leaving was done, I'd do it,
But I never considered death.
"I thought you leaveded me" was so innocently said.
I know you didn't want to go, but leaving is what
    you did.*

Chapter 4
Remembering Mama

Funeral services for Patty JoAnn Larson Wells were Tuesday, November 22, 2005 at Salem Faith Assembly Church in Salem, Missouri. Interment was at North Lawn Cemetery, Salem.

Patty was born September 11, 1942 in Woonsocket, South Dakota to Edward & Phyllis Larson. She married David C. Wells June 26, 1963. She died November 19, 2005 at the age of 63.

Survivors include her husband; three sons, David, Danny and Donnie; and one daughter, Debbie. Four grandchildren. Her father. Four brothers; one sister; several nieces and nephews and host of friends near and far.

Preceding her in death was her daughter, Diana, her mother, two sisters, two brothers, and one brother-in-law.

Mrs. Wells graduated from Salem High School in 1960. She served in many capacities during her life, including piano teacher, cake decorator, 4-H leader, church youth leader, licensed minister, Girl Scout leader, and real estate agent.

Patty was a member of Victory Christian Center in Rolla, Missouri.

FOREVER CHANGED

> We have happy memories of the godly,
> but the name of a wicked person rots away.
> *Proverbs 10:7 (NLT)*

Mama's funeral was beautiful. Since she had meticulously planned almost every detail, I felt even more comforted by the words she asked the pastors to say and the songs she chose to be heard.

Michelle, a friend from Mom's church, opened the service by singing "Beautiful Isle of Somewhere"[1].

Somewhere the sun is shining,

* * * * * * *

Mom loved Swiss Miss mocha-flavored coffee. She would leave a can of it at my house, so that she could have a cup each morning when she visited. I keep the last can she brought in my kitchen cabinet. Next time I clean out the cabinets and reorganize the shelves, I'm sure I'll think, *I really should toss this*, but I can't let it go. I take it out and smell it. It smells like morning at Mom's house.

* * * * * * *

Beautiful Isle of Somewhere!

I had written a poem called "Mama" for her about five years earlier. She proudly displayed the framed copy I had given to her on one of the prominent walls in her home. When she was planning the details of this service, she asked that it be read. Dirk said that he would be honored to do that.

---

[1] Written by Jessie B. Pounds and John S. Fearis

Mama,
You taught me to seek God in everything,
Enjoy the little things in life,
Laugh out loud—even when I'm alone,
Not be afraid of change—sometimes it's good,
Hang in there—even when the going gets tough,
Make everything a learning experience,
Have a good cry every once in a while,
Be a giver who gives good gifts,
Face my fears head on,
Be kind to everyone,
Find the good in people,
Trust my instincts,
Never forget who loves me,
Love all—even those who may need to be knocked down,
Always buy a glass of lemonade from a kid's stand,
Go out for ice cream to celebrate success,
Appreciate nature and true beauty,
Cook—the humming will come later,
Work hard and go for any dream,
Read and write for enjoyment,
Find pictures in the clouds,
Enjoy my own company,
Be proud of my heritage,
Hold my head high,
Be a virtuous woman,
Be a savvy shopper,
Establish fun traditions,
Not sweat the small stuff,
And live life to the fullest.
There's no way that I could ever repay you,
Except to live my life by the virtues you've instilled in me.

As Dirk walked back to his seat, we listened to another song personally selected by Mom: Michael W. Smith's classic recording of "Friends"[2].

Packing up the dreams God planted

* * * * * * *

To know my mother was to know a strong-willed, loving person who had a fun sense of humor and loved drama. She could tell you exactly what was on her mind, whether you liked it or not. She was tough on sin, but gentle on the sinner. She was bold and brassy, yet soft and loving too. She loved deeply and would do all she could for those in need. She was a very positive, joyful person. She had rough things of her own to deal with, but pushed through wanting to make a difference in this world.

Through all of life's hardships, we would hear Mom say, "This, too, shall pass." I like to remind myself of that when I'm feeling frustrated or upset about something.

I miss having a good belly laugh with her. And I miss our inside jokes, the ones that make no sense to outsiders. Laughter was always a common occurrence when we were together.

I miss our shared experiences, our same likes and dislikes, even the differences that we could appreciate in each other.

I miss how we could speak volumes to each other without saying a word.

We were friends.

---

[2] Written by Deborah D. Smith and Michael W. Smith

I miss the way she could comfort me like no other person on earth. I think that is one thing that makes dealing with her death so difficult. In any loss, big or small, she would have been the one to help me through it.

* * * * * * *

That a lifetime's not too long to live as friends.
Pastor Huff came up to talk about my mom and her role in the ladies' ministry at their church.

He began by telling us how Mom had called him up, and told him what she wanted shared. "So," he said, "Patty is still running things, even today."

After he finished, my five-year-old niece Carly came up front to sing "Jesus Loves Me"[3]. Before she began, she proclaimed into the microphone, "This is the best lesson Grandma taught me." It was a precious, precious moment for all of us.

Jesus loves me! This I know,

* * * * * * *

I attended a parenting workshop at our church. The speaker said that "one mark of good parenting is to be open with *faith talk* in front of our children." He defined this as times when we intentionally talk about God, or pray with our kids as needs arise, or talk honestly as we live our faith in front of them.

My mom modeled faith talk so well.

My brothers and I always knew where she was at spiritually. We saw her reading her Bible, and she

---

[3] Written by Anna B. Warner and Wm. B. Bradbury

would quote it to us, if need be. We knew what needs she was praying about.

She laid a solid spiritual foundation in my heart. I knew that she wasn't perfect, but I also knew she was always striving to be more like Christ. It gave me a great, realistic view of what it means to walk with God. I'm convinced that if I hadn't witnessed her faith through her highs and lows first-hand, my own view of Christianity would be quite different. It was her authentic faith that still drives me to be authentic.

* * * * * * *

The Bible tells me so.

Carly returned to her seat, smiling from ear to ear.

Then, my brother Donnie gave us a moment that was meaningful as well.

Mom had asked Donnie to eulogize her. Always the motivator, she told him she was sure he could handle it. He gave the most well-thought-out and loving eulogy I have ever heard. (To honor my brother, I am presenting his comments word-for-word, in their entirety.)

I know that everyone here knows my mom in some way or another. I guess collectively we all knew her pretty well. A person's life is not hidden and that is one reason that death causes us to reflect on life.

My hope here today is to reflect on who my mother really was. For those of you that really know her, you understand how difficult that is. My mother was one of the nicest people that I have ever known. She could also be one of the harshest. She was caring and could meet you wherever you were. She was also very honest and could make you realize your own wrongdoings. My mother met life head on. It was the only direction she knew. I have honestly never seen her back down from any confrontation. She was passionate with everything she did. She was brave, and yet she could turn to tender in an instant. She constantly dreamed of the impossible but was by nature a realist. She was simple enough for anyone to understand, but she could confound the wise with her complexity.

But all of those things are just attributes and cannot possible sum up who my mother really was or what she was really all about. To get closer to who my mother really was I guess you would have to know a couple of stories.

As a child, her world was filled with all the joy and fun that being raised on a farm can bring. She learned early on the difference between livestock and a pet. She became her daddy's little girl learning to gather up the eggs or feed the other animals. She never worked the fields as much because her help was needed around the house with her mother and brothers and sister that would follow. She would help watch her younger brothers Ed, and John and Dave until they were old enough to help work the fields. She also helped with Connie, and Rick and Gary until they sold the farm and moved to Missouri. She always recalled with pride her farming background and always told us her big dream was to someday own a big farm. It was from that farm that she learned the value of hard work. She also learned to love and appreciate gardening. She couldn't have a spring without her plants and flowers in the front of our house, and she loved having a big garden in the backyard.

Her mothering skills came early in life from a promise to her mother to help finish raising the kids. Her *fondest memories in her early married life was helping out with her brothers and sister. She seemed to have been born with the ability to nurture. She loved children so much and always found ways to surround herself with them. It was from this love that she formed a rule of thumb or two. She would say as a rule of thumb when selecting a new church, if the church doesn't have a lot of kids walk out and find a new church. She believed that the children represented the church's commitment to the future. She also surrounded herself with children in countless ways as a Sunday School Teacher, Girl Scout Leader, 4-H Leader, Piano Teacher, Bible Study Leader, Vacation Bible School Volunteer, PTO Homeroom Mother, and Parent and Grandparent Classroom Volunteer.*

Mark 10:13-16 says: [13]People were bringing little children to Jesus. They wanted him to touch them. But the disciples told the people to stop. [14]When Jesus saw this, he rebuked them. He said to his disciples, "Let the little children come to me. Don't keep them away. God's kingdom belongs to people like them. [15]What I'm about to tell you is true. Anyone who will not receive God's kingdom like a little child will never enter it." [16]Then he took the children in his arms. He put his hands on them and blessed them.

My mother's greatest joy came with having a family of her own. That was her role of a lifetime. Not long after her and dad were married in 1963, they began to talk about having children. Mom always said that if she had her way, she would have had six or seven children. Dad and mom always sacrificed so that us kids could have more. Early in their marriage mom worked at Barad's clothing factory. On the side, she ironed clothing and picked up soda bottles to help get ahead. She always knew that through hard work, anything was possible. When dad expressed an interest in auto body, she encouraged him to learn the trade and go into business for himself. She always found a way to bring out the best in people, and she always pushed people to new heights.

My mother knew what it was like to live poor and never forgot those in need. She taught us so much about charity. She couldn't stand to see families who were struggling. I couldn't tell you the number of times mom has gone to our pantry, loaded up bags of groceries and delivered them to families in need. I remember as curious children, we would ask mom why we were giving them our groceries. She would explain that they needed it more than we did and that it was our job to take care of each other.

My mother believed that everyone deserved to be treated fairly. When mom became a real estate agent, she wanted to bring a fresh approach to selling houses. She believed that the smaller sales and commissions deserved as much attention as the big sales and big commissions. Many times people would come to my mom because no one else would help them. My mother never refused anyone the chance to buy a home. Even if they couldn't afford a house she would take them in. She always said, "They deserve to dream big too." She always helped people get what seemed out of reach.

My mom would rent to people that were down on their luck. She never stopped believing in the goodness of people. When renters would get behind in rent, she would find them and before she said anything she would listen to their story. She always said, "Tell me the truth and I will bend over backwards to help you." Those were never empty words either.

When we were children, mom always invited the cousins to the annual cookie bake. Each year we would meet on a Saturday morning and bake cookies for hours. After the cookies were baked we would wrap them and deliver them to homes along with a Christmas carol. The list of people that received these cookies were people that were alone or elderly that would not otherwise have a Christmas. She wanted people to feel loved and wanted.

Matthew 25: 37-40 says: 37Then the righteous will answer him, "Lord, when did we see you hungry and feed you, or thirsty and give you something to drink? 38When did we see you a stranger and invite you in, or needing clothes and clothe you? 39When did we see you sick or in prison and go to visit you?" 40The King will reply, "I tell you the truth, whatever you did for one of the least of these brothers of mine, you did for me."

To really know my mother was to know that she loved South Dakota. The mere mention of South Dakota could make you a friend or foe, depending on what was said. To see her there was to really see her in her element. No matter how much time was spent in Missouri, her home was always South Dakota.

To really know my mother though was to know of her salvation. My mother always credited her first exposure to Christianity from the Moultan's. They were a local pastor's family in South Dakota. They would take her to church and Mrs. Moultan taught her Sunday school. They revealed their Christianity through their lives and how they lived them. That would serve as an example throughout her life. Later in life, in an answer about how she raised her own family, she said that she always wanted to raise her family the way that they had.

Her second and more radical exposure to Christianity would come from her oldest daughter Diana Elaine. Diana was her second-born child born in October

1968, and would die just before reaching her second month in life. It was during the last month of Diana's life that mom began to reflect on her own life and her own mortality. She resolved to help Diana live and made a deal with God. From a Catholic chapel in Cardinal Glennon Children's Hospital she knelt down and prayed, "If you let my daughter live, I will serve you." For the first time in her life, she heard God speak to her heart. And his answer was, "No, I want you to serve me no matter what." Through the death of Diana birthed the realization of what eternal life really is. She understood that if she were ever to see Diana again, it would be through living her life for God. That was where her passion for her Christianity came from.

Matthew 5:14-16 says, [14]You are the light of the world. A city on a hill cannot be hidden. [15]Neither do people light a lamp and put it under a bowl. Instead they put it on its stand, and it gives light to everyone in the house. [16]In the same way, let your light shine before men, that they may see your good deeds and praise your Father in heaven.

The last gift she gave our family ironically was nothing about how she lived. It was how bravely she faced death. That was but one more lesson she demonstrated to us. She wanted to live and see her family grow old, but she also knew that death could not affect her. Death is for those who are not saved. As a Christian, she was ready to transfer from this life to the next life, and that is the true gift of salvation.

1 Corinthians 15:55-57 says, [55]"Where, O death is your victory? Where, O death is your sting?" [56]The sting of death is sin, and the power of sin is the law. [57]But thanks be to God! He gives us the victory through our Lord Jesus Christ.

The truth is we need not idolize my mother or anything that she did but simply remember her for being a great person. Her greatness was the goodness of God.

If today, you think of only one thing, please remember this question. What will they say about you on your day? After a person's life, the things that are said in remembrance are a reflection of that person's greatness. Who my mother was, is the way she lived she lived her life every single day. I would venture a guess there is not one person in this room that knew my mother that was not affected by her. She was very real. She knew who she was. She knew what she wanted out of life. And I guess that is why we all came to her with our concerns and our fears and our problems. And what we got in return was real, genuine, and honest. She was not the one we would go to when we wanted to merely feel better with candy-coated solutions. We came to her when we needed the unaltered blunt in-your-face honesty. And when we came to her that is always what we got.

But somehow what I have written here doesn't seem to say enough. What I have said is not for her, it is for us who must suffer and trudge on through this life. Today is not a sad remembrance of her death; it is a celebration of life. It is a celebration of life because one of God's own fought the good fight and won. It is a celebration of life because with Jesus good does overcome evil. It is a celebration of life because creation will be reunited with its creator. It is a celebration of life because Jesus said if anyone be in Christ, he is a new creature: old things are passed away; behold, all things have become new. It is a celebration of life because we know that if we serve Christ, we will be reunited with her again. But mostly, it is a celebration of life because of the way she lived her life and in the end what else really matters? [sic]

As Donnie finished, a quiet resolve set in. The funeral was progressing just like Mom had planned. She was right. I was happy to know we had done things exactly the way she wanted them to be done.

Bill, a former pastor and family friend, stepped up to share comforting scriptures regarding death from the Bible. My thoughts, however, were somewhere else.

The last dance,
The last chance
To say goodbye.
The last words;
The words unspoken.
The last emotion,
The last look.

Back in 2000, Mom wrote a short essay and submitted it for a newspaper contest. The paper was calling for entries in response to this question: *If you died tomorrow, what would you wish your children would know?* Her entry won $10.

We rediscovered her words as we prepared for the funeral, realizing that she wrote them before she was sick. My brother Danny, home from Africa, read the following out loud to the congregation:

FOREVER CHANGED

Prepare for the Lord
(by Patty Larson Wells)

If suddenly we were no longer together, this is one thing I would want you to carry with you forever. Though sad to leave you, I am not unhappy. You know where I've planned to go since I was small. Now, I leave you this final word.

Prepare every day in every way to join me. This life is only a rehearsal for the real show. First, as you all know, ask Jesus into your hearts and ask Him to forgive your sins. Then, live each day for Him, 'til one day we will all be together forever.

At that point, Danny and Bill presented the Gospel and extended an invitation to receive Christ.

When they finished, we listened to the final song that Mom had chosen just for us: "Days of Elijah" by Robin Mark. I still get goose bumps when I hear this song.

As we left for the graveside service that day, something Mom said came back to me again. "When I'm gone, you'll appreciate knowing that you did things exactly like I wanted." It felt like we had been to an uplifting church service, a true celebration of life, rather than a funeral.

It was perfect.

Last Gifts, Our Inheritance

Out of the many gifts you gave,
The intangible ones stand out the most;

Laughter,
Boldness,
Determination,
Stating exactly what's on your mind,
Not holding back,
Living in the moment,
Heritage and family pride,
Families staying together,
Finding excitement in little things,
Celebrating life's moments,
Devotion.
It brings comfort when we exhibit these traits.
Your last gift to us was a legacy.

> A good man leaves an inheritance [of moral stability and goodness] to his children's children, and the wealth of the sinner [finds its way eventually] into the hands of the righteous, for whom it was laid up.
> *Proverbs 13:22 (AMP)*

"Sis, we'll never pass this way again."

"God always blesses us
beyond our own understanding." – Patty Wells

Layers of uniqueness
rolled into one bold, vibrant, beautiful woman

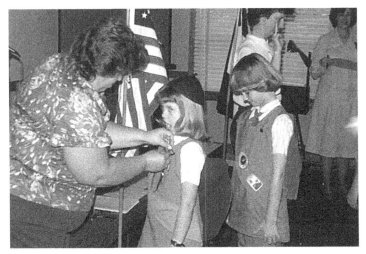

... a sweet remembrance of Mom ...

... and a determination to make her proud
that I am being a good mama, like she was to me

"Give me flowers while I'm alive.
Don't give me any after I'm gone." – Patty Wells

*I didn't know it then—
That it would be our last ride.*

Chapter 5
Surviving the Firsts

There's shock and denial.
Then there's anger.
Next comes depression and detachment,
followed by bargaining and dialogue.
But afterward, finally, acceptance begins to take place.

Thinking back, I'm sure I started grieving when Mom spoke about the "C-word" and said her treatment wasn't going well. But when the actual loss eventually took place, that's when I really felt like I had been run over by a truck. I'm usually a very positive person, but the depression that followed my mother's death was deeper than I could have imagined. It entered my life without permission, and painfully lingered long after I begged for it to leave.

I knew I needed to get from point A—my grief and loss, to point B—healing and healthy living, but I had no clue how to get there. And, boy, did I want to get there fast. I kept thinking, *How would Mom handle this? What would she do?* But, I considered myself less capable and less courageous than I'm sure she had been.

In the weeks following the funeral, I felt numb. I was five and a half months pregnant with our second child, and since I had miscarried our last baby, there was a lot of fear and anxiety with this pregnancy. It only added to the emotional roller coaster I was on at the time. I focused on taking care of my oldest daughter, but found that unwelcome tears would come daily due to my sadness. I would forget to eat and was in an emotional fog. I felt a bit like a robot—going through the motions of life without really living.

One thing that pushed me to get better was the strong desire to honor Mom by not letting depression destroy the rest of my life. I could see her in my mind, with her hands on her hips, saying, "Keep pushing forward, Sis."

A few weeks after Mom died, Dirk decided that I needed to get out of the house for awhile. So we arranged for a babysitter, and he asked what I thought we should do. I told him that a movie sounded like fun. I had been seeing advertisements on television for a movie called "The Family Stone." It looked like there would be a lot of laughs as a crazy family meets the new girlfriend. I thought it would be a perfect escape. Pretty early on though, I realized that movie previews are sometimes misleading. If you've seen it, you know that the story is about a family who is dealing with the fact that their mother has cancer and this might be their last Christmas together. Dirk asked me more than once if I wanted to leave, but I didn't want to move from my seat. I sat there frozen, thinking about how hard it was going to be to have Christmas without Mom. I cried through most of the movie, hoping that this story, unlike my own, would have a happy ending. It didn't, and I was crushed.

For several months, it seemed that every TV show we watched and every movie we rented showed someone dying or featured dialogue about death. I would look over at Dirk, sobbing, as if to say, *Really? Another death theme?* I wondered, *Has death always played a part in this many movies? Is this a coincidence, or am I just more sensitive about it now?*

I found myself crying a lot over the next few months. When I tried to get alone and get quiet, tears would flow freely. I didn't want to cry anymore. I would become angry that I was crying. I would tell my husband that I had surely run out of tears, only to find myself breaking down the next day as well.

Some mornings, as he would leave for work, Dirk would stop and look back at me. He'd say, "I'm really worried about you." I could see the look in his eyes, and I knew that he was really concerned.

I tried to maintain some of my sense of humor and asked if he felt the need to take the sharp knives with him to work that day. While neither of us thinks suicide is funny, it became a familiar joke between us. He would ask about "the knives" when he was particularly worried about my mood.

I never actually felt suicidal, but I was extremely depressed.

* * * * * * *

FOREVER CHANGED

After Mom's death, I spent long weekends at the beginning of each month helping my dad with the paperwork on the rental houses that he and Mom owned. It felt like I was *carrying on* for her.

Those first trips that my young daughter and I made to my hometown weighed heavily on me. The drive itself brought back painful memories. When I passed through the city of Columbia, I couldn't even glance over at the hospital where Mom had received treatments.

It was hard to be in her bedroom, missing her presence in the house I lived in for most of my life. In a way, it was also comforting—smelling her perfumes and seeing her eyeglasses on the nightstand, almost like she had just stepped away for a moment. I found myself strangely drawn to her room. Dad had been sleeping in the guest room ever since Mom got sick. That way, they could both get a better night's rest. After her death, he left their bedroom virtually unchanged. I would just sit on the edge of her bed and take in the smells of her make-up and perfume.

Dad offered to give me items that belonged to Mom. He told me to take whatever I wanted. I took inconsequential things like her voter's card, her key chain, a bottle of her favorite perfume, her cozy sweater.

I needed to feel connected to her.

I put pictures of her in my bedroom, and on my mirror.

I was afraid that, having lost her physically, I might also lose her in every other way. I needed her to stay with me in every way my senses could hold her close—to see her in photographs, to hear her voice in home videos, to smell her perfume, to touch and wear her favorite sweaters and jewelry, to recreate and taste her favorite meals.

I logged on to her email account to see what kinds of emails she was still getting.

Dad and I would sometimes stay up late talking together and crying about Mom. The pain of losing her was much worse for him. His daily routines were now drastically changed. He was alone, and taking it very hard. I was really worried about him.

After Mom's death, I gained a new level of appreciation for the mother she had been to me. Her words carried more weight. Everything she had ever told me, all the lessons she taught me, and the things she had asked me to do before she died became foremost thoughts in my mind.

Holding My Hand

*You were the one holding my hand when I took my
  first steps.
You were there for many bumps and bruises;
  graceful was not my precept.
Whether crossing the street, learning to ride a bike,
  or just taking walks,
It was you, always constant, holding my hand.*

*You were the one holding my hand when I first
    stepped into a scary Kindergarten class.
It seems as though we've blinked and time has
    passed.
Many hard lessons learned along the way, and you
    had to let me learn them.
But, it was you, always constant, holding my hand.*

*You were there holding my hand when I left home
    for the first time.
I wasn't sure I wanted it so.
And oh, how it hurt you when you knew you had to
    let go.
It had to be done; your years of wisdom knew that it
    was best for me.
It was still you, always constant, holding my hand.*

*And on my wedding day, neither of us knew what
    would happen when we let go.
But, we've come to know that we can still be close.
A phone call or letter is like the touch of your hand.
It's been you, always constant, holding my hand.*

*Life is a question with many unspoken answers, but
    through it all, you've been there to guide me.
I'm proud of you, and the dual role you've played as
    both mother and friend.
I don't know what I would have become
If it wasn't for you, always constant, holding my
    hand.*

Days on the calendar that once signaled celebration became days that I found myself dreading.

Our first Christmas without her came only five weeks after Mom's death, and it was a blur.

I woke up the morning we drove back to Salem with the same child-like excitement I always had when we were going home for Christmas. But within a few moments, it hit me hard that Mom was gone, and I broke down. It felt like I was forcing myself into the car to make that trip.

The whole time we were home, I kept thinking that Mom would just come walking out of her bedroom at any moment to join us. Of course, she never did. It seemed like all of my family members were just going through the motions. It was strange that the person who always made Christmas happen for us wasn't around to enjoy it with us.

Feeling lost and alone,
It's much too quiet here.
I can't hear her audible voice,
Though, in my heart, I hear her words.
She was the glue
That held life together.
The bond has changed
For those who knew her.

I wish Mom could have met Kaleah, our second daughter.

About a month before Mom died, Dirk and I had been told that there was a high probability that the baby could have Down's Syndrome. We discussed it and decided not to do any further invasive tests that would tell us for sure.

I cried as I told Mom about the situation. She was confined to bed due to the effects of the chemo she was taking. She reached out her hands, laid them on my belly, and began praying. There was a boldness in her prayer that didn't match her physical appearance. She proclaimed that the baby would be healthy and whole, and spoke Bible verses of healing over my unborn child.

As my March due date was drawing near, however, I was an absolute mess. The night before I was to be induced, I experienced a total meltdown. I was sitting on the floor of my closet, crying and wishing I could hear Mom's comforting voice one more time. Dirk found me there and held me in his arms. He prayed for me and tried to comfort me.

"With God's help," he said, "we can make it through whatever we're facing."

When Kaleah was born late the following afternoon, the first words out of my doctor's mouth were, "Debbie, she's not Downs." I cried bittersweet tears, remembering Mom's prayer for a granddaughter she would never meet.

> TO: A friend
> FROM: Debbie
> DATE: 04/21/06
>
> I've really been missing Mom, and I wish she could share in our joy right now. But, I also have peace that she taught me what I need to know. I can hear her voice in my head when the same things come up with Kaleah that came up with Lynnaya. I used to

> call her at all hours of the day and night, and ask, "What do I do about this or that?" Her words are coming back to me and it's comforting.
>
> She's been gone five months, but it seems like a lot longer—I've heard this first year is the toughest.
>
> I had my six-week post-partum checkup today and I had them run the CA125 "tumor marker test" that can show if things are out of whack—ovarian cancer can be hereditary. I just want to be proactive and not have the attitude that "it can't happen to me." My doctor says it's a good idea because, by the time you have the symptoms of ovarian cancer that could make you go to the doctor, it's usually too late. (My results came back in the normal range.)
>
> Anyway, that's where I'm at right now. I'm trying to learn from Mom's successes (parenting, life in general, etc.) and her mistakes (not taking care of herself and never going to the doctor).

As with many other occasions that first year, I wanted very much for Mom to be there for Kaleah's baby dedication at church. (For us, dedications are less about the baby and more about the parents' decision to raise their child in the Christian faith. Maybe they should be called *parent dedications* instead?) I wrote this poem when we dedicated Kaleah in August.

FOREVER CHANGED

*You should have been there.
She was born a week delayed.
She was beautiful and perfect,
Just the way you prayed.*

*You should have been there
When we brought her home.
My nerves were shot, wondering
If I could go at this alone.*

*You should have been there.
Your words of wisdom had been true;
When big sister welcomed her so sweetly,
My heart was big enough for two.*

*You should have been there—
A phone call away—
Those sleepless nights,
When I needed you to pray.*

*You should have been there
As her personality emerged.
You'd be so proud to know
She's a Larson on the verge.*

*You should have been there.
Her eyes sparkled on stage,
As we dedicated Kaleah Gracyn,
To show her Jesus all of her days.*

You were missed very quietly,
And it seems so wrong
For someone who was the life of the party
To now be reduced to a memory song.

You should have been there.

I wrote this one day when I was dealing with the sadness of not being able to continue the relationship that Mom and I once shared.

I tried to call you,
But you weren't at home.
I wanted to tell you
Something you'd be amused by.

A cute story that I'd read,
A funny thing your granddaughter did,
A tidbit of my day
That we so casually shared before.

I picked up the phone,
But then it hit me hard
That, even though the numbers would work,
You would not be at home.

You were such an integral part
Of my daily world,
A part of my heart, gone.
Missing you …

FOREVER CHANGED

Mom's first birthday after her death was particularly hard for me.

September 11th ... Your Day

*Your day, your birth,
A reason to celebrate.
Gone are the candles and gifts.
Any well wishes are too late.*

*Your gift to me—
A reason to go on—
Is all you taught me
About life and death.*

*I still hear your voice in my head;
Your words I still heed.
I so wish I could talk to you.
I didn't know you were leaving so soon.*

*Forever you will remain
Sixty-three years old.
You won't age a day past;
You'll never grow old.*

*I have regrets
That I didn't celebrate enough.
I should have done more.
Dealing with that is tough.*

This day means nothing to you now—
One thousand years as one day;
One day as a thousand—
I hope the time is passing quickly for you
And not dragging like it is here.

Where are you?
I wonder that often.
I wish I could find peace.

That first year, I found that there are predictable times when I miss Mom more than usual. For instance, her "death-iversary" — my own made-up word for the anniversary of Mom's death. It's just one of the days on the calendar that gives me a sinking feeling deep in my chest. No matter what my state of mind, it always seems to be a day of dread. Just like a lot of things in the grieving process, it can't be avoided. How I have responded and reacted to that day has varied over the years.

Still ...

I still laugh when I think of fun times we shared.
You were so full of life, and adventure always
followed you.

I still start to phone you when there's news to tell,
Forgetting only for an instant that you won't be there
when I call.

FOREVER CHANGED

*I still hope that I did enough while you were on this earth
To show you how deeply I cared.*

*I still wish for five minutes more,
To share all that is happening with my life.*

*I still smile when a memory comes to my mind;
You capitalized on making memories in everyday living.*

*I still wonder why things had to end the way they did;
Perhaps one day the questions will be answered.*

*I still marvel at the person you were;
Layers revealed more amazing now that you're gone.*

*I still hear your voice in my head;
Recalling advice or words of wisdom you shared.*

*I still press on because of the way you raised me;
I know that's what you want me to do.*

*Although time has a way of healing,
I still cry, for the sadness never completely goes away.*

I've learned that I can't promise myself that I won't cry. I can't just pretend certain days don't bother me, because they can sneak up and break my heart anyway. The best way I've found to deal with them is to give myself a lot of slack on those days, and to just let there be fewer rules about the right way to handle things. I know Mom wouldn't want me to be sad and depressed on those days. The first year, I experienced a lot of guilt over being sad, and that wasn't healthy either.

I was somewhat shocked to find that the second year, in some ways, was actually harder for me than the first.

2007

Happy New Year!
At least I hope that is so.
We are now in a year
That doesn't touch the year
Of sorrow in losing you.

Relief in some ways—
Further from the suffering,
Further from the pain,
Further from the wondering
Of what this change would bring.

Sad in some ways—
Further from the memories,
Further from the joys,
Further from the time
We had you in the flesh.
As each year passes,
Will it get easier?
Does that mean we lose
A little of you as each one goes?

FOREVER CHANGED

Are your years passing
As slowly as one thousand of them?
Or quickly, as minutes ticking in a day?

Wherever your spirit is dancing today,
Please know that 2007 will be a year
That we remember you dear in our hearts,
But move on like you would want us to.

As time went by, I felt more removed from Mom. I began to face the reality that she was never coming back. I couldn't pretend that Mom just missed a big event one year, and that she'd be back the second. She really was gone.

Searching desolate fields
For her familiar name.
She's not really there,
But that's where we left her.

Somehow, seeing in stone
What our minds refuse to believe
Makes it more real,
And hurts more,
Because we cannot deny,
We cannot pretend
We're really not searching.

Now, when sad days approach, I intentionally look for ways to honor Mom's memory. I make her favorite breakfast or just enjoy time with my girls. The main goal is to push through those days. I'm always glad when they're over. From time to time, things come up, and it surprises me that there is still hurt in my heart. I can't control when those feelings pop up, but I have learned what I can do with them. I can be grateful for the time I had with my mom. I can be honest with God, and pray something like, "I'm jealous (hurt, bitter, resentful), but I don't want to be. Help me overcome these feelings, Lord, and not let this be a stumbling block in my walk with You. Heal my heart."

Chapter 6
Lynnaya

My little daughter Lynnaya was so, so young when her grandmother died. Sometimes, she would see me cry, even though I tried my best to hold the tears back. That precious little girl would come up to me, put her tiny hands on my cheeks, and say, "Wipe those crocodile tears," an expression I used with her when the need arose.

"You tinkin' about Gamma?" Of course, her sweetness tended to make me cry even more.

I read somewhere that writing down memories for your child is a valuable thing to do. Little ones suffer too, and can be more confused than adults when dealing with the emotions of a loss. They can read your writings when they are older, and get a big picture sense of what they were going through in the time of their grief.

I'm thankful that God used a 2½-year-old little girl to help comfort me when no other person was around. And I still love reading the *Lynnaya stories* that I journaled in the months after Mom's death.

Dear Journal...............................November 21, 2005
Your Grandma Wells' visitation was tonight.
You asked to go look at her body, and asked, "Gamma resting?"
When Daddy and I lifted you up to look, you asked, "Gamma sick?"
"No. Grandma's not sick. She's gone to be with Jesus."
You replied, "Gotta go be with Jesus." Then you said, "I love you, Gamma."

Dear Journal...
Your grandma delighted in everything you came up with. A few days before she died, she said she would regret not getting to see you grow up, because you approached life so differently and she wanted to see how you would turn out.
Please never doubt that Grandma loved you with every fiber of her being. I wish you were older so that you would have memories of her—you two were like two peas in a pod.

Dear Journal...............................February 9, 2006
We were saying our prayers Monday night, and you prayed for all the family members, like we do every night. When you got to Grandpa and

"Grandma up in heaven," you just stopped and looked at me. You asked, "How do we get Grandma back out of the sky?"

I just started crying. Your daddy heard me through the monitor, came running up, and took over our nighttime routine. I just went to my bedroom and cried and cried.

Bless your heart, you asked me again on Tuesday when we were on our way to lunch. I told you that we couldn't get her back, but one day a *long, long* time from now, we will go to heaven and see her.

You asked me again Wednesday, and just looked so sad—it just breaks my heart when I think of a child's simplicity, and how, in your world, you just want to get your grandma back ... like all of the rest of us!

I miss her so much, too. I hope you have memories of her because you two had such a special relationship.

Dear Journal.. May 2006

Right before your third birthday, Grandpa Wells sent a package. We went to the mailbox together to get it.

You asked, "Did Grandma send me a package?"

I answered, "No, sweetie, Grandma can't send you packages because she's in heaven."

You thought for a minute and said, "How are we going to get her down from there?"

I told you we couldn't, and you said, "Maybe Jesus can get her down from there."

You asked me if Grandma was sick in the hospital.

"Not anymore, sweetie."

Then you asked, "Did Jesus heal her?"

I said, "Yes, He did. Jesus gave her the ultimate healing by taking her to heaven." I think, even in your 3-year-old mind, you understood.

Dear Journal ....July 9, 2006

Tonight, while I was giving you a bath, out of the clear blue, you said, "I remember your mom."

I said, "You do? What do you remember?"

"I remember that your mom is my grandma." Then, you went on to say, "I was very special to Grandma."

I could have just cried. If I had one thing I would want you to remember, it is that your grandma loved you and thought you were special.

Later on in the evening, you said, "Let's go look at the stars."

I really didn't want to, and had dishes to do, and you really needed to go to bed ... but I told your daddy, "Mom had an expression for times like these. She would say, 'I brought you into the world. The least I can do is let you show it to me.'"

So, I went out and played with you in Mom's honor tonight, and am so grateful that she showed me how to be a good mom.

Dear Journal.. August 2006

While we were at Grandpa's, you asked if God could give my "big mama" back to her chair. I think you were missing Grandma. In your heart, you just thought we could ask and get her back. I wish it were that simple.

Dear Journal...........................September 11, 2006

Today would have been your Grandma Wells' 64th birthday.

I was sad throughout the day, and you caught me crying. You came up and said, "Do you miss your mom?"

I said, "Yes, sweetie."

Then you said, "Wipe those little crocodile tears," and you reached up and wiped my face.

Then you said, "Remember, I am always here for you." That touched me so much. You are such a sweet and sensitive little thing.

Chapter 7
Always in My Thoughts

There are things in my mind marked *before Mom died*, and things in my mind marked *after Mom died*. Everything in my life is divided into one of these two categories. All of my memories of her are connected with the first; the intense pain of missing her seems to be associated with many moments in the second.

* * * * * * *

There are times during any special event when I miss Mom and wish she could still be a part of our lives here on earth. Sometimes, it's just something that sneaks up on me. Other times, I think of her throughout the entire planning process, as well as during the event.

I wrote this simple poem when we dedicated our third precious daughter. I was dealing, again, with

FOREVER CHANGED

all of the pain of not having Mom there to share the special occasion.

> *I can't put your name on the guest list.*
> *Your presence will not be there.*
> *Mama, she's beautiful.*
> *Her looks are like the Larsons'.*
> *What imprint will I leave on her,*
> *So that your legacy lives on?*
> *How can I explain how you filled*
> *Such a big part of my life,*
> *When you weren't a part of my life*
> *In her lifetime?*

Special times with my girls would often evoke a sadness of heart, mixed with a sweet remembrance of Mom and a determination to make her proud that I am being a good mama, like she was to me.

> *No-Bake Cookies,*
> *Girl Scout ceremony;*
> *Life has come full circle.*
> *Now I'm the mom*
> *And you are gone.*
> *I feel so inadequate.*
> *How did you do it?*
> *You made it look easy.*
> *How will I ever be*
> *The mom I want my girls to remember?*
> *'Cause long after you're gone,*
> *I still remember the little things.*
> *I watched Lynnaya's eyes light up*

As she scanned the crowd and found me.
Smiling so big and proud;
Not too big to hold my hand afterward.
I hope I made you feel as important,
Because you were.
I know I never thanked you enough.
The comprehension was not there.
Only now, as I see myself
Walking in the same paths,
Do I have a glimmer of understanding
Of all you did for me?
So many questions
Still unanswered.
Tears never run out,
Even though they should.
The hurt never completely heals
Like I thought it would.

There were times when I didn't handle my grief very well. Although I never told anyone off, I had some *not so pretty* thoughts along the journey.

I wrote the following when I was pregnant with our third child, and feeling pretty emotional. I seriously considered not including it in this book. However, I want and need to be as transparent as possible. There *is* a private, ugly side to grieving.

What I Want to Say

"Everything's great."
That's what I say,
But that's not what I mean.

FOREVER CHANGED

What I really want to say is,
I miss my mom.
I want her here with me,
To help me through this pregnancy and beyond.

I want to say, "It's not fair
That the happiness I should feel
Is being robbed
Because of the big hole in my heart."

I want to say
That I have many sad moments of missing her,
And wishing that, for one minute,
I could talk to her just one more time.

I wish that I could have her tell me
Everything's going to be okay,
And give me reasons why.

I want to say that my daughter has no issues.
She doesn't lay awake at night missing her grandma.
She wishes for a day that Grandma can "un-die,"
    and come see her.
And ... it's worse that my other children will never
    know her,
And I don't know if I'll do her justice by trying to
    share who she was.

*I want to scream from the top of my lungs
That things will never be okay,
Things will never be normal,
Things will never be completely happy again.
Because there will always be the hurt that she's
	gone,
And never coming back.*

*But, no one wants to listen to all that.
They want to hear that all is well,
That I'm a blissful mother,
Without a care in the world.*

*So, my reply will continue to be,
"Everything's great,"
But that's not what I mean.*

I think we can safely assume that the *Anger* stage of grief was in full bloom there.

I would be lying if I said I handled everything exactly the way I should have, and that my faith wasn't shaken one bit.

I once worked with a woman who had lost her son in a tragic automobile accident. She told me that she quit praying after her son died because it really didn't seem to matter. God was going to do whatever He wanted to do anyway. I was a teenager at the time and was horrified that anyone could entertain those kinds of thoughts. But they were the exact thoughts that came to me after Mom's death.

I don't know of anyone with more faith than my mom. And being in a desperate situation, she was not only praying, but praying for a miracle.

I knew in my heart that I didn't want to go down the road of not having the closeness of prayer in my life, but there were a lot of *whys* regarding Mom's death. There were disappointments and feelings to sort out, so, in my prayers, there was pain.

> My eyes are worn out from crying.
> LORD, I cry out to You all day long;
> I spread out my hands to You. *Psalm 88:9 (HCSB)*

Random Thoughts

I'm finding myself
At a strange place;
Wanting the pain of thinking of you
To go away,
But feeling a closeness
By having the pain.
Is it a betrayal to want
A daily constant nagging loss
To be lessened?
I would never put you on the back shelf,
But I would like the pain to be.
It gets easier,
But it doesn't get easier—
All in the same breath.
'Cause each day you're gone,
There's more of you to miss;
And each day you're gone,
You are further away.
I don't want you to be further away,
I just want this pain to be.

In the summer of 2010, I saw a picture in my hometown newspaper; a picture of Mom's classmates at their 50th reunion. I scanned the faces of her friends, and thought about how much she had always enjoyed being on the reunion committee and helping with the planning. As I recognized the names of her friends, funny stories she had shared about them came to my mind. I wondered if she was missed, because, at least to me, the picture didn't seem complete without her in it.

As crazy as it sounds, I feel a twinge of regret that she didn't get to go to her reunion. I miss that we didn't get to compare notes on how our reunions had gone—my 20th reunion took place earlier that summer. And even though it's just the way things are, I'm sad that life goes on as if nothing ever happened. Only a few close family members and friends seem to understand the feeling and have that nagging pain that never completely fades.

I sat and cried quietly that evening, although I was surprised that I was crying over something that wasn't really that big of a deal. Sometimes, it's the little things.

Once, while traveling by plane with my family, my oldest daughter asked if we'd be close to Grandma in heaven while we were flying above the clouds. I've come to realize that closeness isn't about distance, but rather, connecting the good memories of our loved ones to the little things of today. That's why I feel emotionally close to Mom when I enjoy a good book— especially historical or Christian fiction. When I make one of her recipes for my family or enjoy an activity with my daughters, I feel that she would be proud. I feel close to her when I plant and weed my flowers or spend time baking. She feels close when I spend time with members of her side of the family who share similar characteristics, or I hear one of my daughters' belly laughs. When I have a meaningful dream about her or remember any childhood memory, my heart is full. Certain scents remind me of her. These are moments that, when my eyes are closed, I can almost feel her with me.

When I describe my mom, there's always a fear that I'm not quite getting it right for those who didn't know her. There were so many layers of uniqueness rolled into one bold, vibrant, beautiful woman. She meant the world to me. It's impossible to express the ache in my soul that she is no longer with us here on earth. So, I continue to carry her with me in my heart. She will always be present in my thoughts.

Chapter 8
Moving Forward

*"Joy may seem to pause as grief takes its course,
but those whose broken hearts are bound by Him
will experience it again."*
– Beth Moore
(Praying God's Word Day by Day)

As I was driving with my girls one autumn day, my middle daughter, three-year-old Kaleah, kept pointing out that the trees were "worn out." I asked her what she meant by that, and she described trees with no leaves. She also assured me that it was okay because they would get more leaves.

When I was at my darkest time with grief, I felt like those worn out trees. I felt that there would never be a bright spot again. But with time, and God's amazing healing power, spring does return and we do get more leaves.

I had a beautiful surprise in my yard the spring after Mom died. With all that was happening with Mom, I hadn't followed through with my plans to plant my favorite spring bulbs after we moved into the new house. But as the weather started turning warmer, I was pleasantly surprised to see splashes of color popping up all over my yard. The former owners had chosen my favorite bulbs, flowers and bushes. What a blessing. The daffodils, forsythia, tulips, flox, azaleas, sedum, lilies of the valley, irises, and other spring beauties just delighted me as I noticed each one day-by-day. What a powerful gift from God to bring me those flowers when I was in my deepest grief and pain.

My love of all those flowers came from the yard of my childhood home. Mom had planted the same flowers and bulbs, and I grew up loving them. The experience, although simple to others, was a beautiful manifestation of God's love and beauty shown through His nature. I was so moved that I wrote the former owners and thanked them for all the beauty I was enjoying, and let them know why it was so special for me that year.

* * * * * * *

The summer after Mom died, something unexpected happened. My dad started to have a *special friend* in his life. Her name was Barbara.

I remember the first time Dad told me about her. "If I thought your mom was ever coming back," he said, "you know I'd wait for her. But she isn't, and I need to move on."

My three brothers and I gave him our full support and backing. He had been so depressed until

Barbara came into his life. We were happy that he had decided to move forward.

I got to know Barbara as a very sweet woman—the quiet type. I really appreciated that she wasn't trying to fill the void my mother left. She was simply being a friend.

The second Christmas after Mom's death, Barbara joined us at Dad's for our family's time together. My brothers and I all agreed that it would be a good idea.

It was time to start the family traditions of reading the Christmas story from the Bible and going around the room and telling everyone what we were thankful for. Barbara had excused herself, so she was the last to come into the room. And when she returned, there was only one empty chair—Mom's chair.

In my mind, I was screaming, *Not her chair! Don't sit in Mom's chair!*

Barbara looked over at the empty chair, then walked over to my dad and sat on a small stool that was near him. What a precious deed. I just wasn't ready for Mom's chair to be filled yet.

In the end, Dad kept his end of the deal with Mom. He chose someone who is very good to all of her kids and grandkids. Barbara is a sweet, sweet lady who spoils us rotten. I think Mom would be pleased by his choice.

* * * * * * *

In a lot of ways, Mom's death affected how I view everything. Mother's Day was no exception. It had always been a special day for me to spend with Mom. I am happy that I was able to spend Mom's last

Mother's Day with her. It was a last-minute decision— one that I am so grateful I made.

I decided to take Lynnaya and drive to Salem for the weekend. Mom was not feeling well, but we were able to go and do some things together. We went to Montauk State Park and fed the fish, and then went out for dinner. I bought Mom an orchid corsage to wear to church. Those are memories I will cherish in my heart forever.

After Mom's death, however, Mother's Day was not a happy time at all. For the first three Mother's Day's without her, I was pretty miserable.

Mother's Day

A day set aside to honor,
A day set aside to love,
A day set aside to be together;
It's become a cruel holiday.

I dreaded hearing the commercials on TV about Mother's Day, or seeing card displays at department stores, or hearing people talk about how they were going to spend Mother's Day. When I saw signs in the mall or greeting card aisles beckoning consumers to spoil their mother on Mother's Day, it brought me to tears and could abruptly end a shopping trip.

For three years, it made me too sad to attend church on Mother's Day, to hear a sermon about mothers with a directive to make "mom's day" special. It left me feeling empty, since I didn't have a living mother to whom I could direct my attention and love. It was just too much for me to handle emotionally.

It's important to note that you have to give yourself permission to step aside from doing what's expected sometimes. God knew my heart was breaking, and it wasn't willful disobedience to skip church. It was what I had to do to get through those first few Mother's Days. I knew I would face it eventually, and that was my goal.

I've talked with a lot of people who felt guilty in their grief because they didn't perform the way they did before their loss. But each person has to reach a place where they can allow God to heal them, and that place does not look the same for everyone.

God understands pain and grief. He knew that I had to step out of the norm until I was strong enough emotionally to be back one hundred percent. I think of that time as my "pulling away from the crowds and finding rest," like Jesus Himself did at times (see Luke 5:16 and John 6:15).

In many ways, my grief during Mother's Day robbed me of the joy of celebrating my own motherhood. The change came three and a half years after Mom's death, when it was no longer about being sad all day or trying my best to honor Mom by doing something she enjoyed, which often turned to sadness as well. That year, Dirk and my three beauties brought me breakfast in bed and flowers and cards. It was just a sweet, sweet day for me. That year was a pivotal turning point for me. It was then that I decided to choose joy instead of sorrow. Happiness, in most cases, is a choice. It's clear to me that my girls need a mother to honor on Mother's Day to give them the happy memories that I shared with my mom over the years. Life had come full circle. It was my turn to receive, and their time to give.

Dear Journal .... May 11, 2009

Yesterday was Mother's Day. It was the first one I enjoyed since Mom died. It seems as if I have turned a corner on my grief and am able to enjoy being a mother instead of missing mine so badly.

I had a dream last night that Mom and my three girls were in a big room playing together. Mom was apparently sick, or we had the knowledge that she was. Donnie and I were watching through a window from a nearby house.

I saw Mom get up, and wondered if she was okay. As we kept watching to see if we needed to jump in and help, she was just getting up to get a camera to take a picture of the girls. She was laughing and smiling and enjoying them as only she could do with children!

I stared out the window as if straining to watch her every move, and started crying and saying that I was so worried about her and not ready to lose her.

Donnie comforted me, and said, "She's okay, Deb."

Just then, I was jolted awake upon hearing my youngest child's cry in the monitor. I went into her room to comfort her. As I was rocking her, I cried quietly.

Those dreams always leave me torn. I cry because it's not reality ... but then, I seem to be comforted by it, even though it was a dream.

Mom played with my three girls, and it seemed like that's how it should be and will be someday!

Chapter 9
Spiritual Growth

During my times of deepest grief, it was difficult to read the Bible. It was hard to hear people quote scriptures about healing, or living to an old age, or faith that God can do anything. "Consider it pure joy whenever you face trials" doesn't sit well for someone who is having trouble getting through the day without losing it. Sometimes, however, when I did manage to read the Bible, it was the *comfort* I felt that was too overwhelming. But mostly, I wouldn't read the Bible because I just didn't feel I could handle the raw emotions that came with it.

I don't think that I was falling away from God during those first difficult weeks. I really was leaning on Him like I never had before. To be honest, I had to force myself to start reading the Bible, at first in little chunks. I knew that later I would be able to return to my normal practice of reading the Bible every day.

Although a regular quiet time is important to me, I struggled. I know God understood and that His heart is one of gentle wooing, not Bible thumping.

Going to church was also hard for me the first few months after Mom died. When the praise and worship music would start, my emotions would sometimes overwhelm me. Tears would just come pouring out—the kind that you can't control or make stop. I would be frustrated and embarrassed when the tears came. I hated the feeling of being out-of-control.

When we sang songs about God holding us in His hand, I would feel overwhelmed because I knew that He was the only thing holding me together through the whole chaotic mess.

When we sang about God being able to do anything, how nothing is impossible for Him, I have to admit that I felt some anger and sadness. Those emotions were always followed by guilt about feeling that way.

I've talked to others who have lost loved ones, and many of them say they have experienced the same type of thing. Hearing them talk about the "emotions/guilt over emotions" cycle helped me to feel *less abnormal* about it.

Our church offers Communion on the first weekend of every month. There's a scripture about the seriousness of Communion that I have always been struck by.

> So then, whoever eats the bread or drinks the cup of the Lord in an unworthy manner will be guilty of sinning against the body and blood of the Lord. Everyone ought to examine themselves before they

> eat of the bread and drink from the cup. For those who eat and drink without discerning the body of Christ eat and drink judgment on themselves.
> *1 Corinthians 11:27-29 (NIV)*

It's always been very important to me that my heart is right before God. When I feel that I haven't forgiven someone or I have unsettled feelings, I abstain from taking Communion.

After Mom died, I couldn't take Communion for months, because, like worship music, it caused floods of emotion. I wasn't ready to address the hurt feelings I had. I was like a child who didn't want to be disrespectful to her parents, but didn't understand why she was being punished for some unknown *something*.

I knew God had it in His power to heal my Mom, but for some reason beyond my understanding, He chose not to give her an earthly healing.

> "For My thoughts are not your thoughts, neither are your ways My ways," declares the LORD.
> *Isaiah 55:8 (NIV)*

I was well aware of that verse, but I was still trying to rationalize things in my own mind. I was trying to find a reason for Mom's death, but, for the life of me, I couldn't see what good could come from it. I didn't want to be mad at God, but I just couldn't understand all the *whys*.

It took a while to get to the point where I felt okay to take Communion again.

I was getting ready for church one morning, and was examining my heart. I told God, "I believe my heart is clear and I'm not holding any unforgiveness toward anyone." I was quite proud of myself, and you know what they say about pride going before a fall.

Quietly, God spoke to my heart, and asked, *Have you forgiven Me?* That took me aback for a moment. I was shocked, but then realized that I really had been mad at God, even though I was trying not to be mad at anyone. I had to do some more praying and examining, to figure out where I was with all of it.

I began crying. "Yes, Lord," I said. "I don't want to be mad at You. I wasn't aware that I was angry and unforgiving toward You, but I know now that I was. I don't even know why I held those feelings, Lord. I trust You with Mom's death. I do forgive You. Please, Lord, forgive me."

It's funny how dealings with God are often cyclical, sometimes taking a long time to finally bring closure. My anger with God came up again about two years later.

A friend recommended the book *Boundaries* by Henry Cloud and John Townsend. In addition to being impacted in regard to other relationships in my life, I gained some completely unexpected insight regarding God and how I was dealing with Mom's death.

The authors noted that it's okay to express our anger and disappointment with God. They used Job as an example. He expressed his anger to God, in the context of their relationship, and was not sinning (see Job 1:20-22). It's actually quite healthy to be honest with God, so that He can begin to do His work in our heart. Here are a few of the verses they shared:

> Yet You desired faithfulness even in the womb;
> You taught me wisdom in that secret place.
> *Psalm 51:6 (NIV)*

> Yet a time is coming and has now come when the true worshipers will worship the Father in the Spirit and in truth, for they are the kind of worshipers the Father seeks. God is spirit, and His worshipers must worship in the Spirit and in truth. *John 4:23-24 (NIV)*

For some reason—probably because of my compliant personality—I was trying so hard to not *disappoint* God. I was trying to not be angry with Him over Mom's death, but I was missing the fact that God understands anger, as well as the emotions I entrusted to Him during my grief. Funny how I could express being sad or depressed, but felt guilty for the very human emotion of anger. It took almost four years for me to understand that I could communicate to God that I was angry, as simple as that sounds. With that understanding, though, came more healing and freedom.

There was something else from *Boundaries* that impacted me. It was the idea that we have to respect God's boundaries as well. The story of Jesus' prayer in the Garden of Gethsemane was presented to me in a new light.

Jesus asked His Father to "take this cup of suffering from Me," but as the story continues to unfold, we see that, in essence, the answer was *no*. Think of that. God told His only begotten Son, "No."

When the answer was no to our request that God give us a miracle and heal Mom, He was telling us

Spiritual Growth

that He had other plans. It was another reminder that His ways are not our ways. I can understand that now. I understand that I may not find answers to the *whys* until I reach heaven's gates.

It makes me think of a lyric from an old-time gospel song called "Known Only to Him"[4]; *I know not what the future holds, / But I know who holds the future.*

> My times are in Your hands; ...   Psalm 31:15a (NIV)

My pastor once shared the following quote:

"Adversity does not build character,
it reveals it."
– James Lane Allen

He expressed that, sometimes, we Christians feel that we have earned the right, somehow, to not go through trials. But God is all-knowing and all-powerful, and has our best interest in mind, even when tough times happen in our lives. So, even though it can be very difficult, we really can "Consider it pure joy."

> Consider it pure joy, my brothers and sisters, whenever you face trials of many kinds, because you know that the testing of your faith produces perseverance. Let perseverance finish its work so that you may be mature and complete, not lacking anything.   *James 1:2-4 (NIV)*

---

[4] Written by Stuart Hamblen

During the first few years after Mom's death, I was about as far away from "pure joy" as I could be. But as I healed, I became more willing to admit that I could learn something from the healing process. I could feel God's hand lifting me up.

> Humble yourselves, therefore, under God's mighty hand, that He may lift you up in due time. Cast all your anxiety on Him because He cares for you.
>
> Be alert and of sober mind. Your enemy the devil prowls around like a roaring lion looking for someone to devour. Resist him, standing firm in the faith, because you know that the family of believers throughout the world is undergoing the same kind of sufferings.
>
> And the God of all grace, who called you to His eternal glory in Christ, after you have suffered a little while, will Himself restore you and make you strong, firm and steadfast. To Him be the power for ever and ever. Amen. *1 Peter 5:6-11 (NIV)*

In a book called *One Month to Live*, the authors share how loss can be one of life's most difficult lessons to learn from. They expressed that:

During these times, our faith can be shaken to the core. On one hand, such trials and painful losses force us to depend on God – for comfort, for peace, for His love and mercy. But on the other, we may become angry and resistant to Him because we can't imagine why He would allow such a tragedy, loss or catastrophe in the first place. It's hard to fathom that our freedom of choice comes with one of the steepest price tags imaginable: the sorrow and anguish of an imperfect world. But God never abandons us. He suffers right along with us and knows more than anyone what it means ...   *— Kerry & Chris Shook*

There it was—something key for me to know. Jesus knows what it is to lose someone close. We read about the death of His good friend, Lazarus, in John 11:1-43, and the death of His relative, John the Baptist, in Matthew 14:1-13 and Mark 6:14-30. Jesus loved both of these men, and, even with the knowledge that He would see them again one day, He felt the pain of their earthly deaths. He cried over Lazarus, and was deeply moved when He saw his sister crying. And when He heard that John had been killed, He wanted to be away from the crowds and rest awhile.

I realized, through these stories, that there is no one better to lean on during the grief process than Jesus, since He really does know what it is to grieve. And I also realized that I had moved from not participating in Christian practices to understanding the heart of God a little bit better.

Chapter 10
Receiving Help *from* Others

At first, I didn't share my heart with people outside of my family. It just hurt too much, and pain tends to isolate a person. But when we truly let others into our life, we do become stronger. If it hadn't been for others reaching out to help me, I know my time in the depths of grief would have been much longer. Through people who care about me, I learned that we can't live in a bubble.

When we came home from the funeral, I was overwhelmed by the number of sympathy cards and plants that had been sent by friends offering their condolences. I was grateful for those who offered their help in very tangible ways, to make day-to-day life a little easier. The mother of one of my 20 piano students offered to call the other 19 families and cancel that week's lessons due to my loss. Until she stepped forward, I dreaded the thought of making those calls and repeating my story over and over again.

I had to prepare myself to open the cards I received, and when I did, the tears I cried were due to the love I felt from friends reaching out to me. Certain cards in particular stood out and gave me a lot of comfort. There was something about her beautiful photography on the front and the following scriptures inside that ministered to me and brought me peace.

> ... you will weep and mourn ... You will grieve, but your grief will turn to joy. *John 16:20 (NIV '84)*

> ... weeping may remain for a night,
> but rejoicing comes in the morning.
> *Psalm 30:5b (NIV '84)*

> He will wipe every tear from their eyes. There will be no more death or mourning or crying or pain, for the old order of things has passed away.
> *Revelation 21:4 (NIV '84)*

> You have made known to me the path of life;
> You will fill me with joy in your presence, ...
> *Psalm 16:11a (NIV '84)*

> Praise be to the God and Father of our Lord Jesus Christ, the Father of compassion and the God of all comfort, who comforts us in all our troubles, ... For just as the sufferings of Christ flow over into our lives, so also through Christ our comfort overflows.
> *2 Corinthians 1:3-4a,5 (NIV '84)*

> Do not let your hearts be troubled. Trust in God; trust also in Me. In My Father's house are many rooms; ... I am going there to prepare a place for you. And if I go and prepare a place for you, I will come back and take you to be with Me that you also may be where I am. You know the way to the place where I am going.
>
> ... I am the way and the truth and the life. ...
>
> *John 14:1-4,6 (NIV '84)*

> However, as it is written:
>
> "No eye has seen,
> no ear has heard,
> no mind has conceived
> what God has prepared for those who love Him"—
>
> *1 Corinthians 2:9 (NIV '84)*

Some of the cards I received were from people who I knew had also lost a loved one. Their comfort ministered to me a lot because I was aware that they had experienced the emotions I was feeling.

Other cards were handed to me with the spoken words "I know what you're going through." When I knew that the individual hadn't experienced the loss of a close loved one, this was especially upsetting. About these people, my brother Donnie would say, "They aren't in the club." People would go on and on about how much they loved their mother, so they could understand my pain. This only fostered bitterness in me, not comfort. I would also cringe at clichéd and empty phrases; like "She's in a better place now," "I'm sure your mom is looking down at you right now," or my personal favorite "She'll always be right here with you." It's difficult to tell how someone may be processing their grief, so saying things like this can often do more harm than good.

Job had friends who didn't say the right things to comfort him either.

> Then Job defended himself:
>
> "I've had all I can take of your talk.
>   What a bunch of miserable comforters!
> Is there no end to your windbag speeches?
>   What's your problem that you go on and on like this?
> If you were in my shoes,
>   I could talk just like you.
> I could put together a terrific harangue
>   and really let you have it.
> But I'd never do that. I'd console and comfort,
>   make things better, not worse!"
>
> *Job 16:1-3 (THE MESSAGE)*

It can be difficult for us to know what to say when we are trying to offer comfort to a friend. But here's what I've found: people just being *real* truly means the most. Sometimes, it's as simple as "I have no idea what to say, but I love you." For me, that was always enough. There are no spoken words that can make a loss go away. Our job is not to make it all better, but to just be there and let our friend or loved one know we care.

As Mom's first death-iversary approached, a few of my friends were thoughtful enough to remember the date. They sent me cards reflecting on the person my mom was to them and how much they missed her too. That provided a sweet spot in a day I had dreaded, a day that was otherwise difficult to get through. I now make a point of jotting down these kinds of dates in the lives of my friends, so I can support them on their difficult days. I used to avoid mentioning other people's death-iversaries because I didn't want to make anyone sadder. But the truth is that it's a sad day no matter what. Now, I try to be there for people who have experienced loss, because acknowledging the loss really means valuing the person who is grieving. It helps our hurting friends to know they are not alone.

Throughout my journey, God has blessed me with people being in my life at just the right moment to help with the healing process — different friends with different strengths in the area of comfort. As I said, at first I wasn't ready to talk about my loss, and I had friends who understood that I couldn't rehash everything over and over again. Later, when I wanted to talk about things — probably too much at times, I had faithful friends and family members who would listen to me as I so desperately poured out my heart. I have fond memories now of people who reached out to me when I was feeling all alone in my grief, to let me know they loved me. I will forever be grateful for the wonderful friends God blessed me with along the journey.

Sharon, a woman from my church, obeyed God and started a church small group based on women crocheting together. (The group actually formed a few weeks after Mom died, although I didn't know about it until several months later.) I saw the listing for "Hooked on Life" in our church's small group directory. I called Sharon for the details, and told her that I was a complete beginner who wasn't even sure she could learn to crochet. She was so warm and welcoming. She gave me a list of the materials I would need, and told me several times that she'd be more than happy to show me how to do it. When I attended the group for the first time, Sharon was so patient and loving. She showed me how to crochet in very basic, simple steps. It didn't seem as overwhelming as I thought it would be, and over the next couple of months, I really started to get the hang of it. (Sharon loves to tell people that I took to crocheting so well that I wouldn't put my projects down ... even after going into labor.) Sharon's warmth and caring allowed me to learn to crochet. And God used crocheting to bring me peace and healing, since it had now become another thing I had in common with my mom.

My mom crocheted all the time. I have vivid memories of her sitting in her favorite chair with a crocheting project across her lap. She tried to teach me to do it when I was young, but I just couldn't seem to get the hang of it. She tried again when I was older, but because I had struggled with it before, I really didn't put much effort into learning. After she died, however, I had a strong sense of disappointment about not trying harder so we could share that hobby together. What Sharon and her small group brought into my life was really an answered prayer and some much needed closure. They helped me restore something that could have remained a regret for the rest of my life. I built some wonderful friendships, and gained a sense of pride in accomplishing something I didn't think was possible. And now, because of those women, I feel a connection with Mom every time I sit in my chair with a crocheting project across my lap.

Sometimes, just knowing that others were walking through the journey with me, or that they had been on the same path I was on, would bring me a great deal of comfort. I felt that they truly understood, and I think the desire to understand, and to be understood, is at the heart of our human nature.

Martha, one of Mom's closest friends, was incredibly helpful in those first few weeks and months. She and my mom had been prayer partners for many years. Having lost her own mother, I knew Martha had been where I was. She was so patient with me. I would call her with questions and ask for comforting scriptures. She directed me to specific verses she knew, and each time, they provided the peace and comfort I needed.

The topic of heaven was one that I didn't discuss deeply with Mom, but I did with Martha. Having her share her insights was helpful to me because she and my mom were so in-tune spiritually. I still love and respect Martha's opinions on spiritual matters. Our friendship was another God-ordained connection that helped me to heal.

When a family goes through a death, many things can happen to the structure of that family. For us, Mom had been the hub of the wheel that kept us going. It was interesting to watch different family members step up to fill voids left by her death. Of course, some voids will never be filled. A death can tear a family apart or bring them together. In the case of our family, I think we were drawn closer. Mom surrounded us with a lot of love, so while we continue to move forward with life, we try to honor the traditions and ideas she taught us. Although things aren't exactly the same when we all get together, there's still a lot of laughter and fun.

I gained strength and insight from all of my family members, including Dad, my brothers, and extended family members. But my brother Donnie and I seemed to be *in sync* in the ways we grieved. We seemed to go through the grief cycle in similar patterns. We shared our feelings, thoughts, writings, and emotions with each other, knowing we were experiencing them together. It was a gift to have had a sibling grieving with me each step of the way, one who completely understood. Donnie was one of my biggest cheerleaders when I expressed the idea of writing this book.

Through all of my toughest, grief-filled moments, my husband Dirk has been my rock. He has been such a supportive force throughout this whole journey. He lost his mom when he was only 13, so he had a good grasp of what I was going through. He always listened, never judged, and never seemed to tire of me needing his support.

One year, around the time of Mom's death-iversary, Dirk was downstairs and I was upstairs searching through my binders. I wanted to find just the right poem or writing to share on my Facebook page, to honor Mom. I thought I was crying softly, but my man—the man who can't hear the TV unless it's blaring—heard me and came upstairs to hold me. It was quite a touching moment. I was almost apologizing for my emotions. He said, "You wouldn't be the woman I know and love, if you didn't have that tender heart of yours." Then, he reaffirmed to me that my mom was one in a million.

I looked into his eyes, knowing that my husband—who has been and continues to be my rock—is one in a million. Sometimes, the loss of a loved one can lead to a deepening of the love we hold for those who remain.

Chapter 11
Being There *for* Others

My heart's desire is to comfort those who have lost a parent or loved one. When I hear of someone experiencing a loss like this, I reach out to the person and send comforting Bible verses to them.

> Praise be to the God and Father of our Lord Jesus Christ, the Father of compassion and the God of all comfort, who comforts us in all our troubles, so that we can comfort those in any trouble with the comfort we ourselves receive from God.
> *2 Corinthians 1:3-4 (NIV)*

It's God's plan for us to help each other. Thankfully, there came a time when it started to feel like God could use my journey to help others. Although it brought up memories of my loss, somehow, comforting others strengthened me too.

You Would Be Proud

Today, you would be proud.
I finally get what this trial is for;
To encourage others
Who are going through
What we've been through before.

You lived your life.
You helped others along the way.
You always took responsibility,
And were there for them,
Whatever came their way.

You found a joy
That others miss
When they keep to themselves;
A selfless act of helping
Those in need of bliss.

Your life reflected Christ—
An attitude you acquired.
You "got it" as so many miss
The mission of God's required.

If I had known all along
What your final day would be,
How would it have affected me?
Knowing now, just causes questions
To rise within my soul
Of how I could have done better.
I guess we'll never know.

So, for your life to not be in vain,
We must carry on.
We must pick up your torch.
We must reach out to others.
We must fulfill the Great Commission.

It took a long time for me to really understand that I could be a comfort to others, just as God had sent others to comfort me. They had been there, and they knew what I was going through. Not coincidentally, this is when my healing began. When I reached out to others, that compassion helped to heal me too.

> *"When you dig another out of their troubles,*
> *you find a place to bury your own."*
> *– unknown*

That quote from my childhood rings true with me. It renews my desire to think of others. There's always someone who has a harder road to walk, and reaching out to them is beneficial both to them *and* to us. Personally, helping someone else gives me a sense of gratefulness about my own journey.

> *"Every time we suffer loss,*
> *we have an opportunity for the loss to bring gain*
> *for Jesus' sake*
> *by allowing His life to be revealed."*
> *– Beth Moore*
> *(Praying God's Word Day by Day)*

Those words from Beth Moore challenge me to not let the hurt of Mom's death be in vain, but to allow God to work through me for His glory.

Something as simple as writing a note can help encourage a grieving person. I wrote the following to a close friend who was facing her first set of holidays without her mom.

> Dear friend,
>
> I just wanted you to know that I am thinking of you this week.
>
> The first round of holidays was so hard for me. I felt like I was in a fog and still somewhat in denial. I just kept expecting Mom to "appear" when the family was together, because that's just the way it "should have been."
>
> A couple of things that will help are the love of your family and knowing that your mom would DEFINITELY want you to to hold your chin up and be strong. She'd be getting on to you if you spent the day day upset. (Although, it IS okay to do the best you can to "get through" while maintaining your sanity. That was my goal during that first set of holidays.)
>
> Please know that you are not alone, and that, while it's a tough row to hoe, you're going to be stronger than you thought you could be. It's the inner strength that your mom instilled in you, along with God's comfort, that is going to get you through.

> Also, I found ways to honor my mom on holidays—making her favorite dish, carrying on some of her traditions, enjoying time with my kids in the ways that she did with us, etc. It's a way to feel a connection with her since she can't be there in person with me.
>
> Love, Debbie

Just a simple note, a hug, or word of encouragement can go a long way. I know how much they meant to me. This must be the reason God's word says:

> Be happy with those who are happy, and weep with those who weep.   Romans 12:15 (NLT)

When Jesus walked the earth, His biggest message and His greatest directive was for us to love each other. I believe that God can show His love through us when we love others.

> Jesus replied: "'Love the Lord your God with all your heart and with all your soul and with all your mind.' This is the first and greatest commandment. And the second is like it: 'Love your neighbor as yourself.'"
>   Matthew 22:37-39 (NIV)

As a community of believers, God designed us to reach out to each other and have compassion on those who are hurting.

> So let us seize *and* hold fast *and* retain without wavering the hope we cherish *and* confess *and* our acknowledgement of it, for He who promised is reliable (sure) *and* faithful to His word.
>
> And let us consider *and* give attentive, continuous care to watching over one another, studying how we may stir up (stimulate and incite) to love *and* helpful deeds *and* noble activities, Hebrews 10:23-24 (AMP)

> Finally, all of you, be like-minded, be sympathetic, love one another, be compassionate and humble.
> 1 Peter 3:8 (NIV)

Throughout the grieving process, I learned a lot about accepting love *from* others, which, in turn, helped me become better at giving that kind of love and support *to* others.

Chapter 12
Searching ...

*"The truth of God's love
isn't that He allows bad things to happen,
but that He promises to be there with us through it all.
My daughter could fall down
when I'm walking right beside her.
I'll be there to pick her up,
heal her and rejoice when she's well.
I think that is the Father's love;
He hates to see us suffer,
but wants to be there for us to get through it."
(Love Comes Softly, 20th Century Fox)*

After my mom died, the hardest thing for me was the struggle with the *whys*. After all, God could have given her a miracle. So I found myself searching for comfort and peace in dealing with my grief. I was looking for that new sense of normal. I was looking for joy.

I found books about daughters dealing with their mothers' deaths. I found them, of all places, in Mom's personal library. I realized that, since it was a topic she read about, she must have needed to work through the grief of losing her mom many years earlier.

I believe the loss of a mother is one of the hardest losses for women at any age. I have talked with women in their 60's, and the pain is very intense for them also. No matter our age, or how old our parents are, it's a tough, tough thing.

Most of the books I read made me cry even more. Some even caused me to feel guilty for missing my mom so much. There are daughters who didn't get the chance to say goodbye, if they lost their mother at a very young age, or lost their mom in a single moment. I had to lay some of the books aside until I was ready to read them again.

The title of one of the books in Mom's collection was *Finding the Heart to Go On*. That title served as a mission statement for me for awhile. I would repeat that phrase to myself a lot, and even pray for "the heart to go on."

So, what about all of the unanswered *whys*? Well, that's where faith stepped in. I came to the point where I was able to trust God with my heart. I resolved that there are just certain parts of His plan that we won't know or understand until we meet Him in heaven. He knows the ultimate conclusions to all of our difficulties, and that's okay with me.

When I was able to trust Him, I found that I experienced more peace. It came when I rested on God's sovereignty. It all boiled down to faith in what is to come.

> Now we see things imperfectly, like puzzling reflections in a mirror, but then we will see everything with perfect clarity. All that I know now is partial and incomplete, but then I will know everything completely, just as God now knows me completely.   *1 Corinthians 13:12 (NLT)*

"Christ never allows the hearts of His own to be shattered without excellent reasons and eternal purposes."
— Beth Moore

The above quote, from *Praying God's Word Day by Day*, is from a daily devotional thought dated November 19th—the date of Mom's death. It was as if God hand-picked those words for that day, just to bless me, to comfort me, and to bring me peace.

I came to know that someday there will be answers to my questions. A song by Amy Grant, "Somewhere Down the Road"[5], really spoke to me during that time. The song is a tribute to singer Rich Mullins, who died in a car accident.

Somewhere down the road,
There'll be answers to the questions.
Somewhere down the road,

---

[5] Written by Wayne Kirkpatrick and Amy Grant

Tho' we cannot see it now.
And somewhere down the road,
You will find mighty arms reaching for you —
And they will hold the answers at the end of the road.

It requires a lot of faith to be able to let go of the need for answers, and each person walks a different path to get to that point. Honestly, I believe this is crucial for healing. In my journey, it signified that I had reached the final grief cycle step — *Acceptance.*

> You will seek Me and find *Me* when you search for Me with all your heart. *Jeremiah 29:13 (NASB)*

Chapter 13
Healing ...

God comes to us while we are grieving. Since He shares our grief, we begin to be filled with hope. That's God's amazing healing power.

These are some of Jesus' last words to His disciples:

> Teaching them to observe everything that I have commanded you, and behold, I am with you all the days (perpetually, uniformly, and on every occasion), to the [very] close *and* consummation of the age. *Amen (so let it be).*   Matthew 28:20 (AMP)

It's said that "time heals all wounds." I guess it depends on how you spend the time. There are some who let the loss of a loved one completely destroy their lives. I was determined that this was not going to happen to me.

I believe that if we open our heart to God and allow Him to heal us, He will do it. He is patient and kind, and will wait until we are ready. He is a gentleman. He will not come unless He is invited.

There were times in my grief when I don't think I was open to His healing power. I was too busy trying to fix myself. I think part of that was because of hidden anger and unresolved feelings toward God. I wasn't leaning on Him and trusting His word like I needed to. Even that time was a part of the learning curve for me.

Once I realized that nothing I was doing on my own was working, I invited Jesus in, and asked Him to take away the pain. That is when the true healing began. It took time, of course, but I definitely know that Jesus was the one behind the healing of my wounds.

Part of that healing came through the piano. Sometimes, I would just sit down and play. On one of those occasions, an instrumental melody began to develop around thoughts of Mom's life, her childhood, and the memories we shared of South Dakota. Her home was a part of who she was. It was always pulling at her heart to return. I called the piece "Prairie Girl." (I posted the video of this performance on YouTube — simply search *Prairie Girl Debbie McClure*.)

I played it at my annual recital in 2008, and dedicated it to Mom's memory.

Today's recital is dedicated in memory of my mother, who was my first piano teacher. The song I am playing today is one that I composed in her honor. She was my biggest cheerleader, strongest critic, and a faithful listener. She taught me that, with perseverance, I could achieve any goal, and that anything worth doing is worth doing well.

In addition to my own music, other things also helped:

Journaling. Writing my feelings out—the good, the bad, and the ugly—helped me to deal with them.

Choosing to take care of myself. Mom was stubborn about not going to the doctor. In dealing with her death, there were times when I was angry at her for not taking care of herself. I decided that I would not make the same mistakes. Since Mom's death, I have had the CA125 blood test done every year, during my yearly physical. I also exercise and eat a healthier diet, so I can be around to enjoy my grandchildren.

Finding ways to honor Mom. On days when I can easily be reduced to tears, I find something to do that honors Mom. One Mother's Day, I planted lilac bushes—her favorite—in my back yard.

Donating money or time to charity organizations that Mom cared about.

Reading comforting Bible verses. I've placed a section at the end of this book called *Comfort from Scripture* (Supplement 3) that lists the verses I found helpful throughout my journey.

Keeping a separate journal of memories I'd like my children to know about Mom. One of my fears is that my children will not know Mom for the person she was. Two of my children never met her, and my oldest was very young when she died. I don't want to forget to share things with my children about Mom, so I write them down for them to read.

Reading Mom's own words. Mom wrote a lot of poems, letters, devotions, and short stories about family and life in general. She made it clear that I was to have her case of writings, but asked that I share them with the rest of my siblings. So, for the first Christmas after her death, I gathered copies of everything Mom wrote into huge binders and gave them to my brothers and my dad. It meant a lot to them to have a collection of Mom's writings. My niece, who was five at the time of Mom's death, reads the binder in her spare time as a way to feel connected to her grandma.

Listening to encouraging music. Countless songs have helped me at different times in my grief. Songs like: "Dependence on You" — Jamie Slocum, "Wish You Were Here" — Mark Harris, "Finally Home" — Mercy Me, "Praise You in The Storm" — Casting Crowns, "Still I Will Worship You" — Curt Coffield, "You Never Let Go" — Matt Redman, "Days of Elijah" — Robin Mark, and "Beautiful, Beautiful" — Francesca Battistelli.

When healing began to take place in me, I felt a surge of confidence that I could get through the grief, that there really were brighter days ahead. It was a gradual thing. I didn't wake up one morning and find that everything was all better. In some ways, healing snuck up on me, but when it took place, I felt emotionally stronger than I had before Mom's death. I cannot take the credit for this, though, because the Holy Spirit truly is my Comforter. He proved that God's promises are true.

> I will not leave you comfortless; I will come to you.
> *John 14:18 (KJ21)*

* * * * * * *

My first visits to Mom's gravesite collided with *Denial*—the stage of grief I was experiencing at the time. Seeing her name in stone seemed so final. But that changed over time.

"Give me flowers while I'm alive," Mom would tell my brothers and I. "Don't give me any after I'm gone." She always believed that it didn't matter if you visited gravesites or not, since the person was not really there. She admitted that she used to decorate her baby's grave and her mother's grave just so others didn't think she was a bad person. So, throughout my childhood, I remember only a few times when we took flowers to the grave of a family member.

My brother, Donnie, who visits our hometown only once a year due to distance, usually makes a point to visit Mom's gravesite. He planted a memorial rose garden at his house in Mom's honor, and saves the petals to sprinkle over her grave once a year. I think it's precious, and I enjoy going with him when I can.

These roses are for you, Mom—
Your roses,
Planted in your honor,
Blooming as a reminder
For myself, for others.

These roses are for you, Mom—
Your roses.
Little by little, day by day,
These roses live on
To proclaim your voice.

These roses are for you, Mom—
Your roses;
A lesson you tried to teach others,
A prompting not to let
The little moments pass by.

These roses are for you, Mom—
Your roses;
Your children, your grandchildren.
Even in your death,
Your petals are scattered through each of us.

Four years after Mom's death, I was driving around my hometown with my dad and my youngest daughter Sarayah, who was two at the time. Dad asked if I wanted to visit Mom's grave. When I said yes, it was more for him than me.

As soon as we arrived, Sarayah began innocently dancing on Mom's grave. At first, I was very alarmed, but God actually used that moment to bring about a pivotal closure experience for me.

Quietly and reflectively I stood,
While she began to dance.
My first reaction was to make her stop,
But then I became captivated by her joy.
Her innocence, her unbridled expression—
Gently twirling, swaying and exploring.
A touching moment, although she was unaware.
I saw glimpses of her grandmother,
Who would have shown sheer delight in watching
    her.

Thoughts flooded my mind.
I am amazed at how far I've come,
Standing at the spot where I said my last goodbye,
Finding that my core of pain has slowly faded,
My heart still tender, but not broken.
Joy does comes with the healing;
All part of God's masterful plan.
There was a time to mourn,
But now, it's a time to dance,
So dance, little one, dance!

> You have turned my mourning into joyful dancing. You have taken away my clothes of mourning and clothed me with joy, *Psalm 30:11 (NLT)*

> a time to weep, and a time to laugh;
> a time to mourn, and a time to dance;
> *Ecclesiastes 3:4 (ESV)*

Chapter 14
And Still Learning

I never want to sound like I have *arrived*, because I continue to learn, even now. I am far from perfect. This journey was a new one for me, and I made mistakes along the way. I wish I could tell you that I handled everything with grace and poise, and stood firm on God's promises one hundred percent of the time. I would have loved it if I had never let grief get me down, but the truth is, I think I stumbled and fumbled through every step of my journey.

Even now, years after Mom's death, watching a mother and daughter have a special moment together can bring me to tears. A hug, a knowing look, or a mama still nurturing her grown daughter can put a lump in my throat. I'll admit that, sometimes, there is a bit of jealousy involved.

There were times in the process of writing this book that I would set it on the shelf for long periods of time.

A friend loaned me the book *Battlefield of the Mind* by Joyce Meyer. As I read a chapter called "A Doubtful and Unbelieving Mind," these words struck me:

"Disobedience in a situation
can be giving up when God is prompting us to press on.
Sin is disregarding the voice of the Lord."
— Joyce Meyer

Joyce shared the story from the Bible of Peter walking on the water with Jesus (Matthew 14:24-32). Peter got out of the boat and actually took a few steps on the surface of the water. But, he began to sink because he took his eyes off of Jesus.

I felt a tug on my heart when I read this. It made me realize that God had pressed me to finish this book, but I was letting life and all of its busyness keep me from obeying Him. I had taken my eyes off of Jesus. I repented, asked for forgiveness, and made a decision to continue until I finished this project.

{It's worth noting that, although we read in the Bible that Jesus can calm storms, Peter experienced his miracle *during* the storm. This tells me that the Lord doesn't always change our stormy circumstances. Sometimes, He changes us in the midst of them.}

Some lessons along the way have been harder than others. I somehow thought that, although sorrow is the common lot of man, it happens to others, not me.

That is simply not true. Everyone on this planet will experience some kind of sorrow in their lifetime.

There is an Arabic proverb that says, "All sunshine makes a desert." One of the harder lessons for me was to embrace the rain along with the sunshine, knowing that suffering purifies us and allows us to shine with the love of God. I have learned so much.

Losing my mom opened my heart to what I could have never understood through any other circumstance. It has helped me to reflect on the next world in a way I would never have pondered before. It has given me a sense of compassion for others who are hurting. And it has strengthened my faith that God will walk with me, even hold me, through anything that comes my way.

Would I ever choose to lose my mom? No, but I am now at the point where I can see that God used this experience to teach me so much. Sometimes, God still has to remind me of what I learned in the past, so He can re-teach me to apply it to the present.

It seems that there are lessons all around me.

> *"I walked a mile with Pleasure;*
> *She chatted all the way;*
> *But left me none the wiser*
> *For all she had to say.*
> *I walked a mile with Sorrow;*
> *And ne'er a word said she;*
> *But, oh! The things I learned from her,*
> *When Sorrow walked with me."*
> *— Robert Browning Hamilton*

Chapter 15
The Question of Heaven

I have had a relationship with God ever since I was a little girl, and I have always enjoyed knowing Him personally. At no time during the grieving process did that falter, but ...

After Mom's death, I had a strong desire to know the truth about heaven—the place where my mom was. I would think about it throughout the day, dream about it at night. I would wake up wondering where my mom was right at that moment, and also what it will be like the day we are reunited.

Mom always referred to life as "just the dress rehearsal." She said that the actual performance will be when we are in heaven with Jesus. She explained the concept of heaven this way.

"A toddler playing outside in the sandbox doesn't understand when Mommy carries him in to give him supper and a bath, just as we don't understand being taken from this life. But God knows our needs and has something better for us."

I had never really gotten past the childhood lens of thinking that heaven is a place beyond the clouds where everything is blissful. I simply trusted that God had all the "end of life" stuff figured out, and that was enough.

After Mom died, the desire to thoroughly research what heaven is all about just burned inside me. It was a desire to find comfort. I felt compelled to read what the Bible, and other books, had to say about heaven.

Dirk's aunt suggested that I read Randy Alcorn's book *Heaven*. More of a reference book rather than a cover-to-cover read, it addresses common questions about heaven and offers answers based on Scripture. I found it to be a very thought-provoking book which brought me a lot of peace, so I would recommend it to anyone who is on a similar search.

Based on what I read in the Bible, as well as in other books and commentaries on the subject, here is my personal take on heaven.

When a Christian dies, their spirit goes to paradise — the present version of heaven. *Halley's Bible Handbook* defines paradise as, "a state of conscious blessedness with the Lord."

Paradise is mentioned three times in the Bible.

> Jesus answered him, "I tell you the truth, today you will be with Me in paradise." Luke 23:43 *(NIV '84)*

> ... was caught up to paradise. He heard inexpressible things, things that man is not permitted to tell. *2 Corinthians 12:4 (NIV '84)*

> He who has an ear, let him hear what the Spirit says to the churches. To him who overcomes, I will give the right to eat from the tree of life, which is in the paradise of God. *Revelation 2:7 (NIV '84)*

Paradise cannot be our final destination, though, because of what these verses have to say:

> But let me reveal to you a wonderful secret. We will not all die, but we will all be transformed! It will happen in a moment, in the blink of an eye, when the last trumpet is blown. For when the trumpet sounds, those who have died will be raised to live forever. And we who are living will also be transformed. For our dying bodies must be transformed into bodies that will never die; our mortal bodies must be transformed into immortal bodies. *1 Corinthians 15:51-53 (NLT)*

> Brothers and sisters, we do not want you to be uninformed about those who sleep in death, so that you do not grieve like the rest of mankind, who have no hope. For we believe that Jesus died and rose again, and so we believe that God will bring with Jesus those who have fallen asleep in Him. According to the Lord's word, we tell you that we who are still alive, who are left until the coming of the Lord, will certainly not precede those who have fallen asleep. For the Lord Himself will come down from heaven, with a loud command, with the voice of the archangel and with the trumpet call of God, and

> the dead in Christ will rise first. After that, we who are still alive and are left will be caught up together with them in the clouds to meet the Lord in the air. And so we will be with the Lord forever. Therefore encourage one another with these words.
> *1 Thessalonians 4:13-18 (NIV)*

There are Bible verses that speak of those who have died as "those who have fallen asleep." Some believe that when you die, your soul is asleep until Christ's return, but I cannot accept that idea because of things I found in my research. "Fallen asleep" is a euphemism describing the body's appearance at death.

The following words of Jesus show that those who have died are not sleeping, but very conscious about things.

> There was a rich man who was dressed in purple and fine linen and lived in luxury every day. At his gate was laid a beggar named Lazarus, covered with sores and longing to eat what fell from the rich man's table. Even the dogs came and licked his sores.
>
> The time came when the beggar died and the angels carried him to Abraham's side. The rich man also died and was buried. In Hades, where he was in torment, he looked up and saw Abraham far away, with Lazarus by his side. So he called to him, "Father Abraham, have pity on me and send Lazarus to dip the tip of his finger in water and cool my tongue, because I am in agony in this fire." But Abraham replied, "Son, remember that in your lifetime you received your good things, while Lazarus received bad things, but now he is comforted here and you are in agony. And besides

> all this, between us and you a great chasm has been set in place, so that those who want to go from here to you cannot, nor can anyone cross over from there to us."
>
> He answered, "Then I beg you, father, send Lazarus to my family, for I have five brothers. Let him warn them, so that they will not also come to this place of torment."
>
> Abraham replied, "They have Moses and the Prophets; let them listen to them."
>
> "No, father Abraham," he said, "but if someone from the dead goes to them, they will repent."
>
> He said to him, "If they do not listen to Moses and the Prophets, they will not be convinced even if someone rises from the dead." *Luke 16:19-31 (NIV)*

I found that the Bible mentions a "new earth" in Revelation 21. It is described as the place where God will dwell with people.

> Then I saw "a new heaven and a new earth," for the first heaven and the first earth had passed away, and there was no longer any sea. I saw the Holy City, the new Jerusalem, coming down out of heaven from God, prepared as a bride beautifully dressed for her husband. And I heard a loud voice from the throne saying, "Look! God's dwelling place is now among the people, and He will dwell with them. They will be His people, and God Himself will be with them and be their God. 'He will wipe every tear from their eyes. There will be no more death' or mourning or crying or pain, for the old order of things has passed away." *Revelation 21:1-4 (NIV)*

Although I don't know how all of this will happen, I cannot help but think that seeing New Jerusalem coming down from heaven will be a wondrous sight!

I believe these two places, Paradise and "the new earth," will come together as our final abode. It will be very much like it was when God dwelled in the Garden of Eden before sin.

> ... and by what Christ has done, God has shown us His own mysterious ways. Then when the time is right, God will do all that He has planned, and Christ will bring together everything in heaven and on earth. *Ephesians 1:9-10 (CEV)*

> Heaven must receive Him until the time comes for God to restore everything, as He promised long ago through His holy prophets. *Acts 3:21 (NIV)*

> Peter answered Him, "We have left everything to follow You! What then will there be for us?"
>
> Jesus said to them, "Truly I tell you, at the renewal of all things, when the Son of Man sits on His glorious throne, you who have followed Me will also sit on twelve thrones, judging the twelve tribes of Israel. *Matthew 19:27-28 (NIV)*

Notice how the Bible speaks of restoration and renewal in the scriptures above, instead of a completely different place. For me, that means the final heaven on earth will not seem scary or distant to us, but will be a place that we will be familiar to us. Of course, with the curse of sin removed, it will be better than we could ever imagine. We will also have new, imperishable bodies (see 1 Corinthians 15:35-58), which is an exciting thought!

So, to summarize my research: I believe that Christians who die before the "last trumpet call" (also referred to as the Rapture) will be taken to Paradise. At the Rapture, all Christians will be taken into the new heaven and new earth that God has prepared for us.

I'll borrow my mom's words to re-package my summary into a healthy conclusion: "It doesn't really matter about all the specifics. Just knowing that it will be better than what this world has to offer brings peace enough."

> Christ died for us so that, whether we are dead or alive when He returns, we can live with Him forever.
> 1 Thessalonians 5:10 (NLT)

That verse says it all.

I found that comforting truths about heaven are what allow me to live my life here on earth to the fullest. There is a healthy balance between "being heavenly minded" and "still having an earthly mission" and relevant relationship with God.

I saw a plaque at a department store that read, "Home is where Mom is." My first reaction was the pang of loss that kicks me in the gut because my mom is gone. Then, a resolve set in that, indeed, the phrase is correct. Heavenly-mindedness is the mentality that my eternal home is where my mom and I will be together with Jesus throughout eternity.

Here's a verse that explains the eternal-mindedness of God.

> So we're not giving up. How could we! Even though on the outside it often looks like things are falling apart on us, on the inside, where God is making new life, not a day goes by without His unfolding grace. These hard times are small potatoes compared to the coming good times, the lavish celebration prepared for us. There's far more here than meets the eye. The things we see now are here today, gone tomorrow. But the things we can't see now will last forever. *2 Corinthians 4:16-18 (THE MESSAGE)*

Eventually, I came to the place where I accepted Mom's death and acknowledged that God is God, and that He is sovereign. I now know that His plans are eternally-minded. Once that was settled inside me, I realized that I was not only forever changed by the loss of my mother, but forever changed by the comfort of God as well.

The Bible on Heaven
Supplement 1

> But the Lord is the only true God.
>   He is the living God and the everlasting King!
> The whole earth trembles at His anger.
>   The nations cannot stand up to His wrath.
>
> Say this to those who worship other gods: "Your so-called gods, who did not make the heavens and earth, will vanish from the earth and from under the heavens."
>
> But God made the earth by His power,
>   and He preserves it by His wisdom.
> With His own understanding
>   **He stretched out the heavens**.
>
> *Jeremiah 10:10-12 (NLT)*

> In the beginning God created **the heavens and the earth**.
>
> Then God said, "Let there be an expanse in the midst of the waters, and let it separate the waters

> from the waters." God made the expanse, and separated the waters which were below the expanse from the waters which were above the expanse; and it was so. **God called the expanse heaven.** And there was evening and there was morning, a second day.
> *Genesis 1:1, 6-8 (NASB)*

> Since, then, you have been raised with Christ, set your hearts on things above, where Christ is, seated at the right hand of God. **Set your minds on things above, not on earthly things.** For you died, and your life is now hidden with Christ in God.
> *Colossians 3:1-3 (NIV)*

> **The heavens declare the glory of God;**
>   the skies proclaim the work of His hands.
> Day after day they pour forth speech;
>   night after night they reveal knowledge.
> *Psalm 19:1-2 (NIV)*

> Praise be to the God and Father of our Lord Jesus Christ! In His great mercy He has given us **new birth into a living hope through the resurrection of Jesus Christ** from the dead, and into an inheritance that can never perish, spoil or fade. This inheritance is **kept in heaven for you**, who through faith are shielded by God's power until the coming of the salvation that is ready to be revealed in the last time.
> *1 Peter 1:3-5 (NIV)*

> Praise be to the God and Father of our Lord Jesus Christ, who has **blessed us in the heavenly realms with every spiritual blessing in Christ.** For He chose us in Him before the creation of the world to be holy and blameless in His sight. In love He predestined us for adoption to sonship through

Jesus Christ, in accordance with His pleasure and will—to the praise of His glorious grace, which He has freely given us in the One He loves. In Him we have redemption through His blood, the forgiveness of sins, in accordance with the riches of God's grace that He lavished on us. With all wisdom and understanding, He made known to us the mystery of His will according to His good pleasure, which He purposed in Christ, to be put into effect when the times reach their fulfillment—**to bring unity to all things in heaven and on earth under Christ**.

Ephesians 1:3-10 (NIV)

Then I heard a voice from heaven say, "Write this: **Blessed are the dead who die in the Lord** from now on."

"Yes," says the Spirit, "they will rest from their labor, for their deeds will follow them."

Revelation 14:13 (NIV)

I know a man in Christ who fourteen years ago was caught up to the third heaven. Whether it was in the body or out of the body I do not know—God knows. And I know that this man—whether in the body or apart from the body I do not know, but God knows—was **caught up to paradise** and heard inexpressible things, things that no one is permitted to tell.

2 Corinthians 12:2-4 (NIV)

Jesus said to His disciples, "Don't be worried! Have faith in God and have faith in Me. There are many rooms in My Father's house. I wouldn't tell you this, unless it was true. I am going there to prepare a place for each of you. After I have done this, **I will come back and take you with Me. Then we will be together**.

John 14:1-3 (CEV)

The Bible on Heaven

> **Heaven and earth will pass away**, but My words will never pass away. Matthew 24:35 (NIV)

> But do not forget this one thing, dear friends: With the Lord a day is like a thousand years, and a thousand years are like a day. The Lord is not slow in keeping his promise, as some understand slowness. Instead He is patient with you, not wanting anyone to perish, but everyone to come to repentance.
>
> But the day of the Lord will come like a thief. **The heavens will disappear** with a roar; the elements will be destroyed by fire, and the earth and everything done in it will be laid bare.
>
> Since everything will be destroyed in this way, what kind of people ought you to be? You ought to live holy and godly lives as you look forward to the day of God and speed its coming. That day will bring about the destruction of the heavens by fire, and the elements will melt in the heat. But in keeping with His promise **we are looking forward to a new heaven and a new earth, where righteousness dwells**.
>
> So then, dear friends, since you are looking forward to this, make every effort to be found spotless, blameless and at peace with Him.
> 2 Peter 3:8-14 (NIV)

> For he was looking forward to the city with foundations, **whose architect and builder is God**.
>
> All these people were still living by faith when they died. They did not receive the things promised; they only saw them and welcomed them from a distance, admitting that they were foreigners and strangers on earth. People who say such things show that they

> are looking for a country of their own. If they had been thinking of the country they had left, they would have had opportunity to return. Instead, they were longing for a better country—a heavenly one. Therefore God is not ashamed to be called their God, for He has prepared a city for them.
>
> *Hebrews 11:10, 13-16 (NIV)*

> See, **I will create
> new heavens and a new earth**.
> The former things will not be remembered,
>   nor will they come to mind.   *Isaiah 65:17 (NIV)*

> "As **the new heavens and the new earth that I make will endure before Me**," declares the LORD, "so will your name and descendants endure."
>
> *Isaiah 66:22 (NIV)*

> However, as it is written:
>
> **"What no eye has seen,
> what no ear has heard,
> and what no human mind has conceived"**—
>   **the things God has prepared for those who
>   love Him**—
>
> these are the things God has revealed to us by His Spirit.
>
> The Spirit searches all things, even the deep things of God. For who knows a person's thoughts except their own spirit within them? In the same way no one knows the thoughts of God except the Spirit of God. What we have received is not the spirit of the world, but the Spirit who is from God, so that we may understand what God has freely given us. This is what we speak, not in words taught us by human

The Bible on Heaven

wisdom but in words taught by the Spirit, explaining spiritual realities with Spirit-taught words.
1 Corinthians 2:9-13 (NIV)

Then I saw "**a new heaven and a new earth**," for the first heaven and the first earth had passed away, and there was no longer any sea. I saw the Holy City, the new Jerusalem, coming down out of heaven from God, prepared as a bride beautifully dressed for her husband. And I heard a loud voice from the throne saying, "Look! God's dwelling place is now among the people, and He will dwell with them. They will be His people, and God Himself will be with them and be their God. 'He will wipe every tear from their eyes. There will be no more death' or mourning or crying or pain, for the old order of things has passed away." *Revelation 21:1-4 (NIV)*

The foundations of the city walls were **decorated with every kind of precious stone**. The first foundation was jasper, the second sapphire, the third agate, the fourth emerald, the fifth onyx, the sixth ruby, the seventh chrysolite, the eighth beryl, the ninth topaz, the tenth turquoise, the eleventh jacinth, and the twelfth amethyst. The twelve gates were twelve pearls, each gate made of a single pearl. The great street of the city was of gold, as pure as transparent glass. *Revelation 21:19-21 (NIV)*

No longer will there be any curse. **The throne of God and of the Lamb will be in the city**, and His servants will serve Him. *Revelation 22:3 (NIV)*

Truly I tell you, **anyone who will not receive the kingdom of God like a little child will never enter it**. *Mark 10:15 (NIV)*

Chapter 16
Relationship with Jesus

I know for sure that my mom's relationship with the Lord was the most important thing in the world to her. She trusted Him through thick and thin, and lived that out in front of everyone. She was all about telling others about her relationship with Christ. If you had a pulse, she would reach out and ask, "Do you know where you will spend eternity?"

When I was young, her boldness would embarrass me, because, occasionally, someone would become very vocal in his or her resistance to what she was saying. That never stopped her. Even at the end, she was witnessing to the doctors and nurses who took care of her when she was sick.

She *always* let her light shine bright.

* * * * * * *

Mom began writing a book in 2000, which she hoped to see published one day. She wasn't able to finish it, but from what she wrote, I know what she would want to say to those who haven't made Jesus Christ their personal Lord and Savior yet.

In Mom's own words:

Testimony

I began searching and hungering, and through many trials and errors, stops and starts, I found the Lord, or rather, He found me.

He has worked a lot of things in my life, and He still has a lot to work out in me.

I had a sign in my office that said, "Please be patient with me, God isn't finished with me yet." That is where I am today.

I stand on the following: I would not trade what Jesus Christ is to me for anything or anyone in the world. Through the things I have been through, and the ups and downs in life, I could not have come through them without Jesus.

"Footprints" is a favorite poem to many, especially the part where the man sees only one set of footprints. [He] knows that was a hard time in his life, and asks Jesus, "Why did you leave me when I needed you so?" Jesus answers him and says, "That was when I carried you."

I praise Jesus for carrying me so many times. I give Him all the credit for all the good in my life today. Praise His holy name. He is a great God.

God showed me, one time, that taking someone home is like a child playing in a muddy pool in the middle of the road. A mother would come and rescue the little one from the dangers of the middle of a road. But to the little one taken away, it would seem hard to leave such fun. Before we, or loved ones, are taken, our hearts are all geared up to stay in this mud puddle of life. But God gently rescues us, and takes us home to all [of the] glorious things He has stored up in heaven.

* * * * * * *

Mom wrote the following poem, and its introduction.

God spoke in the Bible of Himself as "I am." I've written this poem as He might speak to us today, telling of how, from [the] beginning of time until now, He speaks to us and cares for us. Listen as if God were speaking to you.

Be Still and Know
(by Patty Larson Wells)

Be still. Be still and know
   That I am your God.
Be still. Be still and know
   That I am your God.

I am the God who was with Adam
Underneath the apple tree.
Whenever sin has victory,
Your heart shall be cleansed by Me.

I am the God who closed the door
When Noah built the boat.

FOREVER CHANGED

*And My hand was gently guiding
To keep it safe afloat.*

*I am the God who comforted Job.
When his life seemed in despair,
But he never would curse Me
Because he knew I cared.*

*I am the God of Abraham,
And the God who loved Isaac,*

*I am the God who stood by Jacob
As he wrestled with a man.
Oh my foolish little children
Don't struggle against My plan.*

*I am the God who led Moses
Up to the promised land.*

*I am the God who sat by Deborah
As she judged Israel under a tree.
I am a God, served by women,
That humbly kneel and pray to Me.*

*I am the God who guided David
As he fought for Israel.
And they're still My chosen people
Though they mended the temple veil.*

*I am the God who came for Elijah
With a chariot that was on fire.
If you delight yourself in Me
I will give you your heart's desire.*

*I am the God who stayed with Jonah
While living in a whale.
I am the God who'll stay by you
Whatever shall prevail.*

*I am the God who walked in the furnace
With Shadrach, Meshach, and Abednego.
And though the flame was seven times hotter
We beheld a pleasant glow.*

*I am the God who went with Daniel
Into the lion's den.
I am the God who'll hold your hand
Till you reach earth's journey's end.*

*I am the God who was with John
When he gave his life for Me.
And when he was beheaded
His spirit became free.*

*I am the God who struck down Saul
With a brilliant light.
When your life is turned to Jesus
Your countenance will be bright.*

*I am the God who spoke to James
And he wrote My word right then.
Even though a brother of your Lord
He, too, was born again.*

*Oh yes, these are ancient ones!
But they placed their hand in Mine.*

The same is true right now
Even in this present time.

And now, I say to you
That this could be the day.
You would turn your life to Me.
My Spirit shows the way.

Just fall upon your knees,
Ask Me to live within your heart.
I do forgive all sins,
And, to you, my love will I impart.

* * * * * * *

In this letter to an unsaved aunt, Mom passionately shares the gospel of Jesus Christ.

I'm not a morning person – hate mornings and love to stay up late, so for me to be up at this hour typing has to be about something else other than "just enjoying being up." That something else is ... **I love you.**
I just woke from a disturbing dream.
In the dream you needed help and I was trying to get to you. You were afraid it was physical help you needed, but I was sure that it was something else.
I know that you might think I am just preaching, but please hear me out. Let me tell you about this, and then, if you want to throw the letter away, go ahead.
When I came to talk at your brother's funeral, and that preacher told about his confirmation, I knew it was going to be hard to say what I wanted to say. Confirmation, baptizing, joining a church, [or] being a member gets you

nothing, unless you have had an experience with God. By that, I mean that you must have a time that you have said to God, "I know that I am a sinner." The Bible says we have all sinned and fallen short of the glory of God.

After that, we must say, "God please forgive me," and, "Jesus, come into my heart." When you say, "Come in," He really comes in and His Spirit abides inside of us.

It's that simple. The churches and religion have made it sound hard and complicated.

If we pray the above prayer, we have prayed "the sinner's prayer." Some call it "getting saved." The book of John calls it "being born again."

If you want to have this experience, but [need] to understand more about it, read the book of John in the New Testament.

John writes, in chapter 3, about Nicodemus, who was a Pharisee – the educated class of people at that time. And he came by night, because he did not want any of his peers knowing he had consulted this unlearned man. Jesus told him he "must be born again."

He said, "How could I return to my mother's womb again?"

Then Jesus told him, "That was a birth of water, but this is a birth of the spirit."

We must all have this birth in order to be in heaven. There is no other way.

Being a good person, doing many good things for others, even giving our life for others does no good. We must be saved or born again. If a good person dies unsaved, it means a good person goes to hell.

People say, "How can a good God send someone to hell?" He doesn't. That's as crazy as saying, How can a good carmaker like Henry Ford make cars to run over and kill people? Henry Ford didn't make cars to kill people. People do it by refusing to drive careful. God doesn't send anyone to hell. We send ourselves by refusing His salvation.

Your daughter can tell you much more if you want to hear it. She is a jewel and really knows the Lord. I know she's had some problems, but being saved doesn't keep problems out of our life, it just gives us someone to turn to when we have problems. The Bible says "many are the afflictions of the righteous," that means saved people, "but the Lord God delivers them out of all of them." God will, and does, answer every prayer we pray.

Please, please consider this. I do not want to think of heaven without any of my uncles and aunts.

Take care, and know [that] I love you, and the Lord really loves you, 'cause He is brave enough to wake me early with you on my heart.

* * * * * * *

I found a few pages of verses that Mom typed out, so she could share the plan of salvation with people—almost a personally-written Gospel tract.

Being Saved, or Born Again

> He saved us, not because of any WORKS or righteous that we had done, but because of His own pity *and* mercy, by [the] cleansing [bath] of the new birth *(regeneration)* and renewing of the Holy Spirit,
>
> Which He poured out [so] richly upon us through Jesus Christ our Saviour.
> [And He did it in order] that we might be justified by His grace (by His favor, wholly undeserved), [that we

might be acknowledged and counted as conformed to the divine will and purpose, thought, and action], and that we might become heirs of eternal life according to [our] hope. *Titus 3:5-7 (AMP)*

For by grace are ye saved through faith; and that not of yourselves: *it is* the gift of God:

Not of works, lest any man should boast.
Ephesians 2:8-9 (KJV)

There was a man of the Pharisees, named Nicodemus, a ruler of the Jews:

The same came to Jesus by night, and said unto Him, "Rabbi, we know that thou art a teacher come from God: for no man can do these miracles that thou doest, except God be with him."

Jesus answered and said unto him, "Verily, verily, I say unto thee, Except a man be born again, he cannot see the kingdom of God."

Nicodemus saith unto Him, "How can a man be born when he is old? can he enter the second time into his mother's womb, and be born?"

Jesus answered, "Verily, verily, I say unto thee, Except a man be born of water and *of* the Spirit, he cannot enter into the kingdom of God.

That which is born of the flesh is flesh; and that which is born of the Spirit is spirit.

Marvel not that I said unto thee, Ye must be born again." *John 3:1-7 (KJV)*

For God so loved the world, that He gave His only begotten Son, that whosoever believeth in Him should not perish, but have everlasting life.

> For God sent not His Son into the world to condemn the world; but that the world through Him might be saved. *John 3:16-17 (KJV)*

> And ye shall know the truth, and the truth shall make you free. *John 8:32 (KJV)*

> If the Son therefore shall make you free, ye shall be free indeed. *John 8:36 (KJV)*

> There is therefore now no condemnation to them which are in Christ Jesus, who walk not after the flesh, but after the Spirit. *Romans 8:1 (KJV)*

> For there is no respect of persons with God. *Romans 2:11 (KJV)*

> That if thou shalt confess with thy mouth the Lord Jesus, and shalt believe in thine heart that God hath raised Him from the dead, thou shalt be saved.
>
> For with the heart man believeth unto righteousness; and with the mouth confession is made unto salvation.
>
> For the scripture saith, Whosoever believeth on Him shall not be ashamed.
>
> For there is no difference between the Jew and the Greek {us}; for the same Lord over all is rich {available} unto all that call upon Him.
>
> For whosoever shall call upon the name of the Lord shall be saved. *Romans 10:9-13 (KJV)*

> So then faith *cometh* by hearing, and hearing by the word of God. *Romans 10:17 (KJV)*

> Neither is there salvation in any other; for there is none other name under heaven given among men, whereby we must be saved. *Acts 4:12 (KJV)*

> Repent ye therefore, and be converted, that your sins may be blotted out, when the times of refreshing shall come from the presence of the Lord; *Acts 3:19 (KJV)*

> … Believe on the Lord Jesus Christ, and thou shalt be saved, and thy house. *Acts 16:31 (KJV)*

> But God commendeth His love toward us, in that, while we were yet sinners, Christ died for us.
>
> Much more then, being now justified by His blood, we shall be saved from wrath through Him. *Romans 5:8-9 (KJV)*

> Let not sin therefore reign in your mortal body, that ye should obey it in the lusts thereof. *Romans 6:12 (KJV)*

> Therefore we are buried with Him by baptism into death: that like as Christ was raised up from the dead by the glory of the Father, even so we also should walk in newness of life. *Romans 6:4 (KJV)*

> For the wages of sin *is* death; but the gift of God *is* eternal life through Jesus Christ our Lord. *Romans 6:23 (KJV)*

> And it shall come to pass, *that* whosoever shall call on the name of the Lord shall be saved. *Acts 2:21 (KJV)*

> Then Peter said unto them, Repent, and be baptized every one of you in the name of Jesus Christ for the remission of sins, and ye shall receive the gift of the Holy Ghost. *Acts 2:38 (KJV)*

> But ye shall receive power, after that the Holy Ghost is come upon you: and ye shall be witnesses unto me both in Jerusalem, and in all Judea, and in Samaria, and unto the uttermost part of the earth. *Acts 1:8 (KJV)*

* * * * * * *

Finally, in this excerpt from a letter written to her then 10-year-old granddaughter, Mom encourages us in how we are to live our life for Christ.

Mom was about to take her second mission trip to Africa—at the age of 62—and was feeling reflective. If something happened and she didn't return, she had things she needed to say as her granddaughter grew into a young woman.

Pray, go to a good Bible-teaching church, and read your Bible every day.

Keep yourself pure and holy.

Do not join the world in what other people want or do. If other people follow "a new thing," then watch out! It might not be the best thing for you.

Remember, pure and holy does not mean that you cannot, or will not, have fun; it just means the sins of the world are not for you. The obvious are [things like] drinking, smoking, stealing, lying, being mean-spirited, and hateful. [But,] it's the unobvious that are bad also, like "what you think in your heart," "what you don't do for others," and that you "only have a religion, not a relationship with God."

God has been my best friend for a long time. I love Him and talk with Him. I joke with Him, fuss with Him, and forget about Him on some days. But, like a best friend, He is always there when I need Him and start talking to Him. That is what a relationship is.

* * * * * * *

Mom had figured out something that others in their entire lifetime here on earth do not. We need to bring along all those we can, so that all will be saved and come into relationship with Jesus.

The Bible on Death and Resurrection
Supplement 2

> Show me, LORD, my life's end
>   and the number of my days;
>   let me know how fleeting my life is.
> You have made my days a mere handbreadth;
>   the span of my years is as nothing before you.
> **Everyone is but a breath**,
>   even those who seem secure.   *Psalm 39:4-5 (NIV)*

> There is a time for everything,
>   and a season for every activity under the heavens:
>
> a time to be born and **a time to die**,
> a time to plant and a time to uproot,
>   *Ecclesiastes 3:1-2 (NIV)*

> and the dust returns to the ground it came from,
> and **the spirit returns to God** who gave it.
>   *Ecclesiastes 12:7 (NIV)*

FOREVER CHANGED

> For to me, to live is Christ and **to die is gain**. If I am to go on living in the body, this will mean fruitful labor for me. Yet what shall I choose? I do not know! I am torn between the two: I desire to depart and be with Christ, which is better by far;
> *Philippians 1:21-23 (NIV)*

> **Precious** in the sight of the LORD
> **is the death of His faithful servants**.
> *Psalm 116:15 (NIV)*

> Jesus said to her, "**I am the resurrection and the life**. The one who believes in Me will live, even though they die; and whoever lives by believing in Me will never die. Do you believe this?"
> *John 11:25-26 (NIV)*

> Since the children have flesh and blood, He too shared in their humanity so that by His death He might break the power of him who holds the power of death—that is, the devil—and **free those who all their lives were held in slavery by their fear of death**.
> *Hebrews 2:14-15 (NIV)*

> **He will swallow up death forever**.
> The Sovereign LORD will wipe away the tears from all faces;
> He will remove His people's disgrace from all the earth.
> The LORD has spoken. *Isaiah 25:8 (NIV)*

> There are also heavenly bodies and there are earthly bodies; but the splendor of the heavenly bodies is one kind, and the splendor of the earthly bodies is another. The sun has one kind of splendor,

the moon another and the stars another; and star differs from star in splendor.

So will it be with the resurrection of the dead. **The body that is sown is perishable, it is raised imperishable**; it is sown in dishonor, it is raised in glory; it is sown in weakness, it is raised in power; it is sown a natural body, it is raised a spiritual body.

If there is a natural body, there is also a spiritual body. So it is written: "The first man Adam became a living being"; the last Adam, a life-giving spirit. The spiritual did not come first, but the natural, and after that the spiritual. The first man was of the dust of the earth; the second man is of heaven. As was the earthly man, so are those who are of the earth; and as is the heavenly man, so also are those who are of heaven. And just as we have borne the image of the earthly man, so shall we bear the image of the heavenly man.

I declare to you, brothers and sisters, that flesh and blood cannot inherit the kingdom of God, nor does the perishable inherit the imperishable. Listen, I tell you a mystery: We will not all sleep, but we will all be changed—in a flash, in the twinkling of an eye, at the last trumpet. For the trumpet will sound, the dead will be raised imperishable, and we will be changed. For the perishable must clothe itself with the imperishable, and the mortal with immortality. When the perishable has been clothed with the imperishable, and the mortal with immortality, then the saying that is written will come true: "**Death has been swallowed up in victory**.

Where, O death, is your victory?
   Where, O death, is your sting?"

> The sting of death is sin, and the power of sin is the law. But thanks be to God! He gives us the victory through our Lord Jesus Christ.
> *1 Corinthians 15:40-57 (NIV)*

> Even though I walk
>   through the valley of the shadow of death,
> I will fear no evil,
>   for **You are with me**;
> Your rod and Your staff,
>   they comfort me.
> *Psalm 23:4 (NIV '84)*

> Therefore we are always confident and know that as long as we are at home in the body we are away from the Lord. For **we live by faith, not by sight**. We are confident, I say, and would prefer to be away from the body and at home with the Lord.
> *2 Corinthians 5:6-8 (NIV)*

Comfort from Scripture
Supplement 3

The following Bible verses really helped me along the way. I found them at various times throughout the grieving process. Whenever I felt down, these verses gave me something to hold on to.

> … "We do not know what to do, but **our eyes are on You**." 2 Chronicles 20:12b *(NIV)*

> Though He brings grief, He will show compassion,
>   so great is His unfailing love.
> For **He does not willingly bring affliction
>   or grief to anyone**. Lamentations 3:32-33 *(NIV)*

> Yet this I call to mind
>   and therefore I have hope:
>
> **Because of the LORD's great love we are not
>   consumed,**

> for His compassions never fail.
> They are new every morning;
> great is Your faithfulness.
> *Lamentations 3:21-23 (NIV)*

> So that they should seek God, in the hope that they might feel after Him and find Him, although **He is not far from each one of us**. *Acts 17:27 (AMP)*

> The Lord is good,
> a strong refuge when trouble comes.
> **He is close to those who trust in Him**.
> *Nahum 1:7 (NLT)*

> Love the Lord, all of you who are faithful to Him!
> **The Lord watches over the faithful**.
> But He completely pays back those who are proud.
> Be strong, all of you who put your hope in the Lord.
> Never give up. *Psalm 31:23-24 (NIrV)*

> Blessed be the Lord—
> day after day He carries us along.
> He's our Savior, our God, oh yes!
> **He's God-for-us, He's God-who-saves-us**.
> Lord God knows all
> death's ins and outs. *Psalm 68:19 (THE MESSAGE)*

> One thing God has spoken,
> two things I have heard
> that **You, O God, are strong
> and You, O Lord, are loving**.
> Surely You reward each person
> according to what he has done.
> *Psalm 62:11-12 (NIV '84)*

> God *is* our refuge and strength,
> **A very present help in trouble.** Psalm 46:1 (NKJV)

> The Lord is a shelter for the oppressed,
>   **a refuge in times of trouble.**
> Those who know Your name trust in You,
>   for You, O Lord, do not abandon those who search
>   for You. Psalm 9:9-10 (NLT)

> But the salvation of the righteous *is* from the Lord;
>   *He is* their **strength in the time of trouble.**
> Psalm 37:39 (NKJV)

> My flesh and my heart may fail,
>   but **God is the strength of my heart**
>   **and my portion forever.** Psalm 73:26 (NIV)

> **Search me, God, and know my heart**;
>   test me and know my anxious thoughts.
> Psalm 139:23 (NIV)

> **Cast your cares on the Lord**
>   and He will sustain you;
> He will never let
>   the righteous be shaken. Psalm 55:22 (NIV)

> Therefore, since we have a great high priest who has ascended into heaven, Jesus the Son of God, let us hold firmly to the faith we profess. For we do not have a high priest who is unable to empathize with our weaknesses, but we have One who has been tempted in every way, just as we are—yet He did not sin. Let us then approach God's throne of grace with confidence, so that **we may receive**

> mercy and find grace to help us in our time of need. *Hebrews 4:14-16 (NIV)*

> Therefore, my dear brothers and sisters, **stand firm. Let nothing move you**. Always give yourselves fully to the work of the Lord, because you know that your labor in the Lord is not in vain.
> *1 Corinthians 15:58 (NIV)*

> Trust God from the bottom of your heart;
>   don't try to figure out everything on your own.
> **Listen for God's voice in everything you do**,
>   everywhere you go;
> He's the One who will keep you on track.
> *Proverbs 3:5-6 (THE MESSAGE)*

> "Don't be afraid, I've redeemed you.
>   I've called your name. You're mine.
> When you're in over your head, **I'll be there with you**.
>   When you're in rough waters, you will not go down.
> When you're between a rock and a hard place,
>   it won't be a dead end—
> Because I am God, your personal God,
>   The Holy of Israel, your Savior.
> I paid a huge price for you …
> That's how much you mean to me!
>   That's how much I love you!
> I'd sell off the whole world to get you back,
>   trade the creation just for you.
> *Isaiah 43:1b-4 (THE MESSAGE)*

> He will wipe every tear from their eyes. **There will be no more death or mourning or crying or pain**, for the old order of things has passed away.
> *Revelation 21:4 (NIV)*

> Do not fear, for I am with you;
> do not be afraid, for I am your God.
> I will strengthen you; I will help you;
> **I will hold on to you** with My righteous right hand.
> *Isaiah 41:10 (HCSB)*

> I cry out to God Most High,
> to **God who will fulfill His purpose for me**.
> *Psalm 57:2 (NLT)*

> I have told you these things, so that in Me you may have peace. **In this world you will have trouble. But take heart! I have overcome the world**.
> *John 16:33 (NIV)*

> for everyone born of God overcomes the world. This is the **victory that has overcome the world**, even our faith.
> *1 John 5:4 (NIV)*

> And God's peace [shall be yours, that tranquil state of a soul assured of its salvation through Christ, and so fearing nothing from God and being content with its earthly lot of whatever sort that is, that **peace] which transcends all understanding shall garrison** *and* **mount guard over your hearts and minds in Christ Jesus.**
> *Philippians 4:7 (AMP)*

> Don't let your hearts be troubled. Trust in God, and trust also in Me.

> I am leaving you with a gift—peace of mind and heart. And **the peace I give is a gift the world cannot give.** So don't be troubled or afraid.
> *John 14:1, 27 (NLT)*

> For this is what the LORD says:
>
> "I will extend peace to her like a river,
> and the wealth of nations like a flooding stream;
> you will nurse and be carried on her arm
> and dandled on her knees.
> **As a mother comforts her child,
> so will I comfort you;**
> and you will be comforted over Jerusalem."
> *Isaiah 66:12-13 (NIV)*

> Praise be to the God and Father of our Lord Jesus Christ, the Father of compassion and the God of all comfort, **who comforts us in all our troubles**, so that we can comfort those in any trouble with the comfort we ourselves receive from God.
> *2 Corinthians 1:3-4 (NIV)*

> The eyes of the LORD are on the righteous,
>   and His ears are attentive to their cry;
>   but the face of the LORD is against those who do
>   evil,
> to blot out their name from the earth.
>
> The righteous cry out, and the LORD hears them;
>   He delivers them from all their troubles.
> The LORD is close to the brokenhearted
>   and saves those who are crushed in spirit.
>
> The righteous person may have many troubles,
>   but **the LORD delivers him from them all;**
> *Psalm 34:15-19 (NIV)*

> Don't be obsessed with getting more material things. Be relaxed with what you have. Since God assured us, **"I'll never let you down**, never walk off and leave you," we can boldly quote,
>
> > God is there, ready to help;
> > I'm fearless no matter what.
> > Who or what can get to me?
> >
> > *Hebrews 13:5-6 (THE MESSAGE)*

> … [He] is able to do **immeasurably more than all we ask or imagine,** according to His power that is at work within us, *Ephesians 3:20 (NIV)*

> I remain confident of this:
> > **I will see the goodness of the LORD
> > in the land of the living.**
>
> Wait for the LORD;
> > be strong and take heart
> > and wait for the LORD. *Psalm 27:13-14 (NIV)*

> When I am hurting,
>
> > **I find comfort in your promise**
>
> > **that leads to life**. *Psalm 119:50 (CEV)*

> … you will weep and mourn … You will grieve, but **your grief will turn to joy**. *John 16:20 (NIV)*

> **Consider it pure joy**, my brothers and sisters, whenever you face trials of many kinds, because you know that the testing of your faith produces perseverance. Let perseverance finish its work so that you may be mature and complete, not lacking anything. *James 1:2-4 (NIV)*

> May our Lord Jesus Christ Himself and God our Father, who loved us and by His grace **gave us eternal encouragement and good hope**, encourage your hearts and strengthen you in every good deed and word.   *2 Thessalonians 2:16-17 (NIV)*

> I consider that our **present sufferings are not worth comparing with the glory** that will be revealed in us.   *Romans 8:18 (NIV)*

> There is a time for everything,
>   and a season for every activity under the heavens:
>
>   a time to weep and a time to laugh,
>   **a time to mourn and a time to dance,**
>   *Ecclesiastes 3:1, 4 (NIV)*

> Those who plant in tears
>   will **harvest with shouts of joy**.
> They weep as they go to plant their seed,
>   but they sing as they return with the harvest.
>   *Psalm 126:5-6 (NLT)*

> As the deer longs for streams of water,
>   so I long for You, O God.
> I thirst for God, the living God.
>   When can I go and stand before Him?
> Day and night I have only tears for food,
>   while my enemies continually taunt me, saying,
>   "Where is this God of yours?"
>
> My heart is breaking
>   as I remember how it used to be:
> I walked among the crowds of worshipers,
>   leading a great procession to the house of God,
> singing for joy and giving thanks
>   amid the sound of a great celebration!

> Why am I discouraged?
>   Why is my heart so sad?
> **I will put my hope in God!**
>   I will praise Him again—
>   my Savior and my God! *Psalm 42:1-5 (NLT)*

> **The LORD bless you and keep you;**
> The LORD make His face shine upon you,
> And be gracious to you;
> The LORD lift up His countenance upon you,
> And give you peace. *Numbers 6:24-26 (NKJV)*

Through every emotion and experience I had after Mom's death, one thing remained constant. I knew God was with me. My testimony can be summed up with these words:

> If God hadn't been there for me,
>   I never would have made it.
> The minute I said, "I'm slipping, I'm falling,"
>   Your love, God, took hold and held me fast.
> When I was upset and beside myself,
>   **You calmed me down and cheered me up.**
>   *Psalm 94:17-19 (THE MESSAGE)*

Comfort from Scripture

Appendix 1
Scripture Version Copyrights

Scripture quotations marked (NIV '84) are taken from the Holy Bible, New International Version®. Copyright © 1973, 1978, 1984 by International Bible Society.

Scripture quotations marked (NIV) are taken from the Holy Bible, New International Version®, NIV®. Copyright © 1973, 1978, 1984, 2011 by Biblica, Inc.™ Used by permission of Zondervan. All rights reserved worldwide. (www.Zondervan.com)

The "NIV" and "New International Version" are trademarks registered in the United States Patent and Trademark Office by Biblica, Inc.™

Scripture quotations marked (KJV) are taken from the King James Version, Public Domain.

Scripture quotations marked (NLT) are taken from the Holy Bible, New Living Translation, copyright © 1996, 2004, 2007 by Tyndale House Foundation. Used by permission of Tyndale House Publishers, Inc., Carol Stream, Illinois 60188. All rights reserved.

Scripture quotations from *THE MESSAGE*. Copyright © by Eugene H. Peterson 1993, 1994, 1995, 1996, 2000, 2001, 2002. Used by permission of NavPress Publishing Group.

Scripture quotations marked (AMP) are taken from the *Amplified Bible*, Copyright © 1954, 1958, 1962, 1964, 1965, 1987 by The Lockman Foundation. Used by permission.

Scripture quotations marked (NKJV) are taken from the New King James Version. Copyright © 1982 by Thomas Nelson, Inc. Used by permission. All rights reserved.

Scripture quotations marked (CEV) are from the Contemporary English Version Copyright © 1991, 1992, 1995 by American Bible Society. Used by permission.

Scripture quotations marked (HCSB) are taken from the Holman Christian Standard Bible®, Copyright © 1999, 2000, 2002, 2003 by Holman Bible Publishers. Used by permission. Holman Christian Standard Bible®, Holman CSB®, and HCSB® are federally registered trademarks of Holman Bible Publishers.

Scripture quotations marked (KJ21) are taken from the 21st Century King James Version®, copyright © 1994. Used by permission of Deuel Enterprises, Inc., Gary, SD 57237. All rights reserved.

Scripture quotations marked (NIrV) are taken from the Holy Bible, New International Reader's Version®, NIrV® Copyright © 1995, 1996, 1998 by Biblica, Inc.™ Used by permission of Zondervan. All rights reserved worldwide. (www.Zondervan.com)

The "NIrV" and "New International Reader's Version" are trademarks registered in the United States Patent and Trademark Office by Biblica, Inc.™

Appendix 2
Index of Debbie's Poems

{Poem titles appear in capital letters; first lines in upper and lower case letters.}

Written	Title / First line	Pages
1998-ish	**HOLDING MY HAND**	47/48
12/25/2000	**MAMA**♥	25
12/3/2004	**I wished for you**	3/4
Early 2006	**I tried to call you**	53
8/20/2006	**You should have been there**	52/53
9/11/2006	**SEPTEMBER 11th ... YOUR DAY**	54/55
11/22/2006	**I cooked the Thanksgiving meal**	21/22
12/15/2006	**YOU WOULD BE PROUD**	102/103
1/1/2007	**2007**	57/58
Feb. 2007	**Searching desolate fields**	58

♥ "Mama" is presented on page 25 in a *figure* Debbie refers to as "Mom with Outstretched Arms." It replicates the framed copy her mother proudly displayed in her home.

Written	Title / First line	Pages
2/21/2007	**Feeling lost and alone**	49
5/12/2007	**MOTHER'S DAY**	78
6/11/2007	**WHAT I WANT TO SAY**	69-71
11/19/2007	**STILL …**	55/56
1/25/2008	**These roses are for you, Mom**	115/116
Apr. 2008	**I can't put your name on the guest list**	68
5/10/2008	**LAST GIFTS, OUR INHERITANCE**	37
5/10/2008	**The last dance**	35
6/4/2008	**RANDOM THOUGHTS**	72
7/12/2008	**OUR LAST RIDE**	6/7
11/11/2008	**No-Bake Cookies**	68/69
12/10/2009	**Quietly and reflectively I stood**	116/117

In addition to Debbie's writings, three creative writings by Patty Larson Wells (Debbie's mom) appear in this book.

Title	Pages
THE GIRL IN MY LIFE	19-21
PREPARE FOR THE LORD	36
BE STILL AND KNOW	139-142

Made in the USA
Middletown, DE
10 April 2020